UML 2.0

IN A NUTSHELL

Other resources from O'Reilly

Related titles   Learning UML   C++ in a Nutshell
                      UML Pocket Reference   Head First Design Patterns

oreilly.com   *oreilly.com* is more than a complete catalog of O'Reilly books. You'll also find links to news, events, articles, sample chapters, weblogs, and code examples.

oreillynet.com is the essential portal for developers interested in open and emerging technologies, including new platforms, programming languages, and operating systems.

Conferences   O'Reilly brings diverse innovators together to nurture the ideas that spark revolutionary industries. We specialize in documenting the latest tools and systems, translating the innovator's knowledge into useful skills for those in the trenches. Visit *conferences.oreilly.com* for our upcoming events.

Safari Bookshelf (*safari.oreilly.com*) is the premier online reference library for programmers and IT professionals. Conduct searches across more than 1,000 books. Subscribers can zero in on answers to time-critical questions in a matter of seconds. Read the books on your Bookshelf from cover to cover or simply flip to the page you need. Try it today with a free trial.

UML 2.0

IN A NUTSHELL

Dan Pilone
with Neil Pitman

O'REILLY®

Beijing · Cambridge · Farnham · Köln · Paris · Sebastopol · Taipei · Tokyo

UML 2.0 in a Nutshell

by Dan Pilone with Neil Pitman

Published by O'Reilly Media, Inc., 1005 Gravenstein Highway North, Sebastopol, CA 95472.

O'Reilly books may be purchased for educational, business, or sales promotional use. Online editions are also available for most titles (*safari.oreilly.com*). For more information, contact our corporate/institutional sales department: (800) 998-9938 or *corporate@oreilly.com*.

Editor:	Jonathan Gennick
Production Editor:	Mary Anne Weeks Mayo
Cover Designer:	Ellie Volckhausen
Interior Designer:	David Futato

Printing History:

June 2005:	First Edition.

 This book uses RepKover™, a durable and flexible lay-flat binding.

ISBN: 0-596-00795-7

[M]

For my family: the reason I wrote this book and the reason I was able to.

—Dan Pilone

For Laurie Ann:
Giorraíonn beirt bóthar/Two people shorten the road.

—Neil Pitman

Table of Contents

Preface

About This Book

Welcome to *UML 2.0 in a Nutshell*. The Unified Modeling Language (UML) has expanded quite a bit since its inception and can be applied to many different domains, however it still has its roots in software development. We have tried to make this book applicable to as broad an audience as possible, but it's helpful to have at least a cursory knowledge of Object Oriented Programming (OOP) because UML draws much of its terminology from that domain.

Before going any further we'd like to clarify how this book refers to the Unified Modeling Language. Grammatically speaking, "the UML" is correct. However, it sounds weird. This book uses the more colloquial "UML".

UML 2.0 in a Nutshell is a detailed reference for the UML 2.0 Superstructure, from a user's perspective. Whenever it would be helpful to clarify a UML concept with a concrete example, we will present Java code.

In general we assume that you are familiar with OOP and the type of constructs that go with it (classes, methods, inheritance, etc.). However, we make no assumptions about what you know about UML. Each chapter starts with a top-to-bottom discussion of the chapter's topic. This will be fast paced and thorough, meant for those who understand the basics and want to know the "nitty-gritty" of a piece of UML. Subsequent sections are kinder, gentler discussions of the topic. This includes examples that show how the topic may be applied to typical problems, help you further refine your models to eliminate ambiguity, capture details that might otherwise be lost, or add information to your model that aids in tool-based development.

A brief word of warning: UML has a strict terminology for just about every aspect of modeling. This is necessary to reduce ambiguity and confusion as much as possible. However, in everyday use some terms are used interchangeably with others that have completely different meanings in UML. A classic example of this is operation and method. These are frequently treated as being synonymous in a software development environment but have different meanings when used in the context of UML. We will make a point to use the correct UML term even if it may not be the most colloquial name.

How to Use This Book

This book is divided based on UML diagram type. Obviously there is some cross-over, as some diagrams build on concepts from others. Chapter 1, *Fundamentals of UML*, covers the basics of UML and presents some background information that will help you understand the context for the rest of the book. If you are familiar with previous versions of UML, you can probably skim this chapter. If you don't have a strong background in UML, you should definitely start here.

The next set of chapters cover what is called static modeling in UML. Static modeling captures the physical structure of a piece of software (as much as software has a "physical" structure). For example: what operations and attributes a class contains, what interfaces a class realizes, or what packages contain all this mess. The static modeling chapters include:

Chapter 2, *Class Diagrams*
> This chapter introduces the class diagram. It discusses the various elements that can be used on a class diagram, what they represent, and how to extend them. Because class diagrams are often a centerpiece of a UML model, you should know this chapter inside and out. The last part of the chapter discusses how class diagrams fit into the overall UML model and how the diagrams are typically mapped to code.

Chapter 3, *Package Diagrams*
> This chapter introduces packages and grouping within a UML model.

Chapter 4, *Composite Structures*
> This chapter introduces the new UML 2.0 concept of composite structures. Composite structures are specifically designed to represent patterns and are a major new component to the modeling language.

Chapter 5, *Component Diagrams*
> This chapter introduces components and the component diagram. Topics such as the stereotypes used in component diagrams, relationships between components, and component metainformation are discussed. The latter part of this chapter discusses how components are typically realized in a programming language.

Chapter 6, *Deployment Diagrams*
> This chapter introduces the concept of capturing system deployment using deployment diagrams. Deployment fundamentals such as nodes, node stereotypes, and relationships to components are explained. This chapter also includes a discussion on modeling a distributed system using deployment diagrams.

The next set of chapters cover the second half of UML—behavioral modeling. Behavioral modeling captures how the various elements of a system interact during execution. Diagrams such as the use case diagram can capture requirements from an external actor's perspective, and sequence diagrams can show how objects interact to implement a particular use case. The behavioral modeling chapters include:

Chapter 7, *Use Case Diagrams*
>   This chapter introduces use cases, actors, and system boundaries. It goes slightly beyond pure UML in that the chapter touches on common practices regarding use cases, such as use case scoping, use case documents, and use case realizations.

Chapter 8, *Statechart Diagrams*
>   This chapter introduces state machine modeling using states, actions, and transitions. Statecharts can be used to model a simple algorithm all the way up to a complex system.

Chapter 9, *Activity Diagrams*
>   This chapter introduces a close relative to the statechart diagram, the activity diagram. Activity diagrams resemble old-school flowcharts and are typically used to model an algorithm or use case realization.

Chapter 10, *Interaction Diagrams*
>   This chapter introduces the large set of interaction diagrams supported by UML 2.0. The two best-known diagrams are sequence and collaboration diagrams. This chapter also discusses the new timing-centric interaction diagram.

The final part of the book covers extension and applications of UML 2.0:

Chapter 11, *Tagged Values, Stereotypes, and UML Profiles*
>   This chapter discusses how UML 2.0 may be extended and refined.

Chapter 12, *Effective Diagramming*
>   This chapter departs from the specification side of UML 2.0 and offers real-world advice on modeling, what parts of UML 2.0 to use when, and how to effectively convey the right information.

Appendix A, *MDA: Model-Driven Architecture*
>   This appendix introduces the Model-Driven Architecture (MDA). While MDA isn't a new idea, UML 2.0 has MDA in mind in several places, and next-generation tools may be able to make MDA a reality.

Appendix B, *The Object Constraint Language*
>   This appendix describes the Object Constraint Language (OCL), a simple language defined to express constraints on UML diagrams. It can be applied in countless ways and is introduced here in its basic form.

If you're familiar with the fundamental UML concepts, you can read this book's chapters in nearly any order. However, there is always a certain amount of overlap between chapters because some elements can appear on many diagrams. Instead of repeating the information in each chapter, we fully define elements (and their associated stereotypes, attributes, etc.) the first time they are encountered, and in subsequent chapters, we provide detailed cross references back to the original definition, when needed.

Typographic Conventions

The following typographic conventions are used in this book:

`Constant width`
> Used in the text to refer to class names, stereotypes, and other elements taken from UML diagrams.

`Constant width italic`
> Used in UML diagrams to indicate text that would be replaced by the user.

Italic
> Used when new terms are introduced, and for URLs and file references.

...
> Ellipses indicate nonessential material that has been omitted from a diagram for the sake of readability.

Indicates a tip, suggestion, or general note.

Indicates an aspect of UML that you must be particularly careful about using.

Note that UML makes frequent use of curly braces ({}) and guillemots («»). When these are used in a syntax definition, they are required by UML.

Nearly everything in UML notation is optional, so there is no specific notation to indicate an optional field. If a particular piece of syntax is required, it is noted in the text.

Safari Enabled

When you see a Safari® Enabled icon on the cover of your favorite technology book, it means the book is available online through the O'Reilly Network Safari Bookshelf.

Safari offers a solution that's better than e-books. It's a virtual library that lets you easily search thousands of top tech books, cut and paste code samples, download chapters, and find quick answers when you need the most accurate, current information. Try it for free at *http://safari.oreilly.com*.

Comments and Questions

Please address comments and questions concerning this book to the publisher:

> O'Reilly Media, Inc.
> 1005 Gravenstein Highway North
> Sebastopol, CA 95472
> 800-998-9938 (in the United States or Canada)

707-829-0515 (international/local)
707-829-0104 (fax)

There is a web page for this book that lists errata, examples, or any additional information. You can access this page at:

http://www.oreilly.com/catalog/umlnut2

To comment or ask technical questions about this book, send email to:

bookquestions@oreilly.com

For more information about books, conferences, Resource Centers, and the O'Reilly Network, see the O'Reilly web site at:

http://www.oreilly.com

Acknowledgments

From Dan

This book was truly a team effort. Without support, emails, comments, harassment, and suggestions from friends, family, and colleagues, this book would not have happened. First I'd like to thank my editor, Jonathan Gennick, for his astonishing amount of patience. He is fantastic to work with and helped keep this book on track.

Next, I'd like to thank the technical reviewers who were never short on suggestions or comments. At times I felt like this was the fourth edition of the book, after working in all their ideas. The tech reviewers were: Stephen Mellor, Michael Chonoles, Mike Hudson, Bernie Thuman, Kimberly Hamilton, Russ Miles, and Julie Webster.

Finally, I'd like to thank my family: my parents for supporting me from the start and setting an example that has driven me in both my professional and personal life, and my wife, Tracey, for somehow managing to hold everything together while I wrote this book. Compared to the magic she has been working, writing this book was a piece of cake. Last but not least, I'd like to thank my son Vinny: now we can head to the park!

From Neil

I'd like to thank Ron Wheeler and Jacques Hamel of Artifact-Software for allowing the use of XML examples. Thanks also to Derek McKee of Mindset Corporation for the use of LamMDA examples. Finally, I'd like to especially thank Jonathan Gennick for his depth of patience.

Fundamentals of UML

On the surface, the Unified Modeling Language (UML) is a visual language for capturing software designs and patterns. Dig a little deeper, though, and you'll find that UML can be applied to quite a few different areas and can capture and communicate everything from company organization to business processes to distributed enterprise software. It is intended to be a common way of capturing and expressing relationships, behaviors, and high-level ideas in a notation that's easy to learn and efficient to write. UML is visual; just about everything in it has a graphical representation. Throughout this book we'll discuss the meaning behind the various UML elements as well as their representations.

Getting Started

If you're new to UML, you should be sure to read this chapter all the way through to get acquainted with the basic terminology used throughout the book. If you are a developer, class diagrams tend to be the simplest diagrams to start with because they map closely to code. Pick a program or domain you know well, and try to capture the entities involved using classes. Once you're convinced you've modeled the relationships between your entities correctly, pick a piece of functionality and try to model that using a sequence diagram and your classes.

If you're more of a process person (business or otherwise), you may be more comfortable starting with an activity diagram. Chapter 9 shows examples of modeling business processes with different groups (Human Resources, IT, etc.) and progresses to modeling parallel processes over different geographic regions.

Background

UML has become the de facto standard for modeling software applications and is growing in popularity in modeling other domains. Its roots go back to three distinct methods: the Booch Method by Grady Booch, the Object Modeling

Technique coauthored by James Rumbaugh, and Objectory by Ivar Jacobson. Known as the Three Amigos, Booch, Rumbaugh, and Jacobson kicked off what became the first version of UML, in 1994. In 1997, UML was accepted by the Object Management Group (OMG) and released as UML v1.1.

Since then, UML has gone through several revisions and refinements leading up to the current 2.0 release. Each revision has tried to address problems and shortcomings identified in the previous versions, leading to an interesting expansion and contraction of the language. UML 2.0 is by far the largest UML specification in terms of page count (the superstructure alone is over 600 pages), but it represents the cleanest, most compact version of UML yet.

UML Basics

First and foremost, it is important to understand that UML is a *language*. This means it has both syntax and semantics. When you model a concept in UML, there are rules regarding how the elements can be put together and what it means when they are organized in a certain way. UML is intended not only to be a pictorial representation of a concept, but also to tell you something about its context. How does widget 1 relate to widget 2? When a customer orders something from you, how should the transaction be handled? How does the system support fault tolerance and security?

You can apply UML in any number of ways, but common uses include:

* Designing software
* Communicating software or business processes
* Capturing details about a system for requirements or analysis
* Documenting an existing system, process, or organization

UML has been applied to countless domains, including:

* Banking and investment sectors
* Health care
* Defense
* Distributed computing
* Embedded systems
* Retail sales and supply

The basic building block of UML is a diagram. There are several types, some with very specific purposes (timing diagrams) and some with more generic uses (class diagrams). The following sections touch on some of the major ways UML has been employed. The diagrams mentioned in each section are by no means confined to that section. If a particular diagram helps you convey your message you should use it; this is one of the basic tenants of UML modeling.

Designing Software

Because UML grew out of the software development domain, it's not surprising that's where it still finds its greatest use. When applied to software, UML attempts to bridge the gap between the original idea for a piece of software and its implementation. UML provides a way to capture and discuss requirements at the requirements level (use case diagrams), sometimes a novel concept for developers. There are diagrams to capture what parts of the software realize certain requirements (collaboration diagrams). There are diagrams to capture exactly *how* those parts of the system realize their requirements (sequence and statechart diagrams). Finally there are diagrams to show how everything fits together and executes (component and deployment diagrams).

Books describing previous versions of UML made a point to emphasize that UML was not a visual programming language; you couldn't execute your model. However, UML 2.0 changes the rules somewhat. One of the major motivations for the move from UML 1.5 to UML 2.0 was to add the ability for modelers to capture more system behavior and increase tool automation. A relatively new technique called Model Driven Architecture (MDA) offers the potential to develop executable models that tools can link together and to raise the level of abstraction above traditional programming languages. UML 2.0 is central to the MDA effort.

It is important to realize the UML is *not* a software process. It is meant to be used within a software process and has facets clearly intended to be part of an iterative development approach.

While UML was designed to accommodate automated design tools, it wasn't intended *only* for tools. Professional whiteboarders were kept in mind when UML was designed, so the language lends itself to quick sketches and capturing "back of the napkin" type designs.

Business Process Modeling

UML has an extensive vocabulary for capturing behavior and process flow. Activity diagrams and statecharts can be used to capture business processes involving individuals, internal groups, or even entire organizations. UML 2.0 has notation that helps model geographic boundaries (activity partitions), worker responsibilities (swim lanes), and complex transactions (statechart diagrams).

UML Specifications

Physically, UML is a set of specifications from the OMG. UML 2.0 is distributed as four specifications: the Diagram Interchange Specification, the UML Infrastructure, the UML Superstructure, and the Object Constraint Language (OCL). All of these specifications are available from the OMG web site, *http://www.omg.org*.

The Diagram Interchange Specification was written to provide a way to share UML models between different modeling tools. Previous versions of UML defined an XML schema for capturing what elements were used in a UML diagram, but did not capture any information about how a diagram was laid out. To address this, the Diagram Interchange Specification was developed along with a mapping from a new XML schema to a Scalable Vector Graphics (SVG) representation. Typically the Diagram Interchange Specification is used only by tool vendors, though the OMG makes an effort to include "whiteboard tools."

The UML Infrastructure defines the fundamental, low-level, core, bottom-most concepts in UML; the infrastructure is a metamodel that is used to produce the rest of UML. The infrastructure isn't typically used by an end user, but it provides the foundation for the UML Superstructure.

The UML Superstructure is the formal definition of the elements of UML, and it weighs in at over 600 pages. This is the authority on all that is UML, at least as far as the OMG is concerned. The superstructure documentation is typically used by tool vendors and those writing books on UML, though some effort has been made to make it human readable.

The OCL specification defines a simple language for writing constraints and expressions for elements in a model. The OCL is often brought into play when you specify UML for a particular domain and need to restrict the allowable values for a parameter or object. Appendix B is an overview of the OCL.

It is important to realize that while the specification is the definitive source of the *formal definition* of UML, it is by no means the be-all and end-all of UML. UML is designed to be extended and interpreted depending on the domain, user, and specific application. There is enough wiggle room in the specification to fit a data center through it... this is intentional. For example, there are typically two or more ways to represent a UML concept depending on what looks best in your diagram or what part of a concept you wish to emphasize. You may choose to represent a particular element using an in-house notation; this is perfectly acceptable as far as UML is concerned. However, you must be careful when using nonstandard notation because part of the reason for using UML in the first place is to have a common representation when collaborating with other users.

Putting UML to Work

A UML model provides a view of a system—often just one of many views needed to actually build or document the complete system. Users new to UML can fall into the trap of trying to model everything about their system with a single diagram and end up missing critical information. Or, at the other extreme, they may try to incorporate every possible UML diagram into their model, thereby overcomplicating things and creating a maintenance nightmare.

Becoming proficient with UML means understanding what each diagram has to offer and knowing when to apply it. There will be many times when a concept could be expressed using any number of diagrams; pick the one(s) that will mean the most to your users.

Each chapter of this book describes a type of diagram and gives examples of its use. There are times when you may need to have more than one diagram to capture all the relevant details for a single part of your system. For example, you may need a statechart diagram to show how an embedded controller processes input from a user as well as a timing diagram to show how the controller interacts with the rest of the system as a result of that input.

You should also consider your audience when creating models. A test engineer may not care about the low-level implementation (sequence diagram) of a component, only the external interfaces it offers (component diagram). Be sure to consider who will be using each diagram you produce and make it meaningful to that person.

UML Profiles

In addition to a variety of diagram types, UML is designed to be extended. You can informally extend UML by adding constraints, stereotypes, tagged values, and notes to your models, or you can use the formal UML extension and define a full *UML profile*. A UML profile is a collection of stereotypes and constraints on elements that map the otherwise generic UML to a specific problem domain or implementation. For example, there are profiles for CORBA, Enterprise Application Integration (EAI), fault tolerance, database modeling, and testing. See Chapter 11 for more information on UML 2.0 Profiles.

Modeling

It should go without saying that the focus of UML is modeling. However, what that means, exactly, can be an open-ended question. Modeling is a means to capture ideas, relationships, decisions, and requirements in a well-defined notation that can be applied to many different domains. Modeling not only means different things to different people, but also it can use different pieces of UML depending on what you are trying to convey.

In general a UML model is made up of one or more *diagrams*. A diagram graphically represents things, and the relationships between these things. These things can be representations of real-world objects, pure software constructs, or a description of the behavior of some other object. It is common for an individual thing to show up on multiple diagrams; each diagram represents a particular interest, or *view*, of the thing being modeled.

Diagrams

UML 2.0 divides diagrams into two categories: *structural diagrams* and *behavioral diagrams*. Structural diagrams are used to capture the physical organization of the things in your system—i.e., how one object relates to another. There are several structural diagrams in UML 2.0:

Class diagrams
> Class diagrams use classes and interfaces to capture details about the entities that make up your system and the static relationships between them. Class diagrams are one of the most commonly used UML diagrams, and they vary in detail from fully fleshed-out and able to generate source code to quick sketches on whiteboards and napkins. Class diagrams are discussed in Chapter 2.

Component diagrams
> Component diagrams show the organization and dependencies involved in the implementation of a system. They can group smaller elements, such as classes, into larger, deployable pieces. How much detail you use in component diagrams varies depending on what you are trying to show. Some people

simply show the final, deployable version of a system, and others show what functionality is provided by a particular component and how it realizes its functionality internally. Component diagrams are discussed in Chapter 5.

Composite structure diagrams

Composite structure diagrams are new to UML 2.0. As systems become more complex, the relationships between elements grow in complexity as well. Conceptually, composite structure diagrams link class diagrams and component diagrams; they don't emphasize the design detail that class diagrams do or the implementation detail that composite structures do. Instead, composite structures show how elements in the system combine to realize complex patterns. Composite structures are discussed in Chapter 4.

Deployment diagrams

Deployment diagrams show how your system is actually executed and assigned to various pieces of hardware. You typically use deployment diagrams to show how components are configured at runtime. Deployment diagrams are discussed in Chapter 6.

Package diagrams

Package diagrams are really special types of class diagrams. They use the same notation but their focus is on how classes and interfaces are grouped together. Package diagrams are discussed in Chapter 3.

Object diagrams

Object diagrams use the same syntax as class diagrams and show how actual instances of classes are related at a specific instance of time. You use object diagrams to show snapshots of the relationships in your system at runtime. Object diagrams are discussed as part of class diagrams in Chapter 2.

Behavioral diagrams focus on the behavior of elements in a system. For example, you can use behavioral diagrams to capture requirements, operations, and internal state changes for elements. The behavioral diagrams are:

Activity diagrams

Activity diagrams capture the flow from one behavior or *activity*, to the next. They are similar in concept to a classic flowchart, but are much more expressive. Activity diagrams are discussed in Chapter 9.

Communication diagrams

Communication diagrams are a type of interaction diagram that focuses on the elements involved in a particular behavior and what messages they pass back and forth. Communication diagrams emphasize the objects involved more than the order and nature of the messages exchanged. Communication diagrams are discussed as part of interaction diagrams in Chapter 10.

Interaction overview diagrams

Interaction overview diagrams are simplified versions of activity diagrams. Instead of emphasizing the activity at each step, interaction overview diagrams emphasize which element or elements are involved in performing that activity. The UML specification describes interaction diagrams as emphasizing who has the *focus of control* throughout the execution of a system. Interaction overview diagrams are discussed as part of interaction diagrams in Chapter 10.

Sequence diagrams

> Sequence diagrams are a type of interaction diagram that emphasize the type and order of messages passed between elements during execution. Sequence diagrams are the most common type of interaction diagram and are very intuitive to new users of UML. Sequence diagrams are discussed as part of interaction diagrams in Chapter 10.

State machine diagrams

> State machine diagrams capture the internal state transitions of an element. The element could be as small as a single class or as large as the entire system. State machine diagrams are commonly used to model embedded systems and protocol specifications or implementations. State machine diagrams are discussed in Chapter 8.

Timing diagrams

> Timing diagrams are a type of interaction diagram that emphasize detailed timing specifications for messages. They are often used to model real-time systems such as satellite communication or hardware handshaking. They have specific notation to indicate how long a system has to process or respond to messages, and how external interruptions are factored into execution. Timing diagrams are discussed as part of interaction diagrams in Chapter 10.

Use case diagrams

> Use case diagrams capture functional requirements for a system. They provide an implementation-independent view of what a system is supposed to do and allow the modeler to focus on user needs rather than realization details. Use case diagrams are discussed in Chapter 7.

Views

While not strictly part of UML itself, the concept of *views of a system* helps the modeler choose diagrams that help convey the correct information depending on his goals. Specifically, models are often divided into what is called the *4+1 views* of a system. The 4+1 notation represents four distinct views of a system and one overview of how everything fits together. The four views are:

Design view

> The design view captures the classes, interfaces, and patterns that describe the representation of the problem domain and how the software will be built to address it. The design view almost always uses class diagrams, object diagrams, activity diagrams, composite structure diagrams, and sequence diagrams to convey the design of a system. The design view typically doesn't address how the system will be implemented or executed.

Deployment view

> The deployment view captures how a system is configured, installed, and executed. It often consists of component diagrams, deployment diagrams, and interaction diagrams. The deployment view captures how the physical

layout of the hardware communicates to execute the system, and can be used to show failover, redundancy, and network topology.

Implementation view

The implementation view emphasizes the components, files, and resources used by a system. Typically the implementation view focuses on the configuration management of a system; what components depend on what, what source files implement what classes, etc. Implementation views almost always use one or more component diagrams and may include interaction diagrams, statechart diagrams, and composite structure diagrams.

Process view

The process view of a system is intended to capture concurrency, performance, and scalability information. Process views often use some form of interaction diagrams and activity diagrams to show how a system actually behaves at runtime.

The four distinct views of a system are brought together with the final view:

Use case view

The use case view captures the functionality required by the end users. The concept of end users is deliberately broad in the use case view; they include the primary stakeholders, the system administrator, the testers, and potentially the developers themselves. The use case view is often broken down into collaborations that link a use case with one or more of the four basic views. The use case view includes use case diagrams and typically uses several interaction diagrams to show use case details.

Notes

UML provides a catchall element, or note, for adding information to your diagram. The note symbol is a dog-eared rectangle with an optional dashed line to link it to some element. Figure 1-1 shows a simple note.

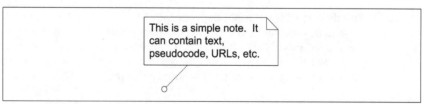

Figure 1-1. A simple note

In general, you can use notes to capture just about anything in your diagram. Notes are often used to express additional information that either doesn't have its own notation or would clutter a diagram if you drew it right on the element. Some tools allow you to embed URL links in notes, providing an easy way to navigate from one diagram to the next, or to HTML documents, etc.

Classifiers and Adornments

The basic modeling element in UML is the *classifier*. A classifier represents a group of things with common properties. Remember, at the level of classifier, we are discussing UML itself, not a particular system. So, when we say a *class* is a classifier, we mean that *classes* are things that have common properties: methods, attributes, exceptions, visibility, etc. A specific class, such as Automobile, isn't a UML classifier; it's an instance of a classifier, or a class.

 For the truly self-abusing, this is a glimpse into the UML *metamodel*. The full metamodel is quite complex and begins with the UML infrastructure specification.

A classifier's generic notation is a rectangle that can be divided into *compartments* to show classifier-specific information, such as operations, attributes, or state activities. However, many UML classifiers such as states, activities, objects, etc., have custom notations to help distinguish them visually.

A classifier can have several types of extra information attached to it via a UML mechanism called *adornments*. For example, classifiers can have restrictions placed on the values a feature of the classifier can take. In general, constraints are written near the classifier or in an attached note. See the specific diagram types for details on what notation to use for a constraint when writing it near the classifier.

Another type of adornment is a *stereotype*. Just as you would expect, a stereotype is intended to give the reader a general idea of what a particular classifier represents. Stereotypes are usually associated with implementation concepts, such as «transactional» or «singleton», though that isn't required by the UML specification.

UML Rules of Thumb

While UML provides a common language for capturing functionality and design information, it is deliberately open-ended to allow for the flexibility needed to model different domains. There are several rules of thumb to keep in mind when using UML:

Nearly everything in UML is optional. UML provides a language to capture information that varies greatly depending on the domain of the problem. In doing that, there are often parts of UML that either don't apply to your particular problem or may not lend anything to the particular view you are trying to convey. It is important to realize that you don't need to use every part of UML in every model you create. Possibly even more importantly, you don't need to use every allowable symbol for a diagram type in every diagram you create. Show only what helps clarify the message you are trying to convey, and leave off what you don't need. At times there is more than one way to convey the same information; use what is familiar to your audience.

UML models are rarely complete. As a consequence of everything being optional, it is common for a UML model to be missing some details about a system.

The trick is to not miss key details that could impact your system design. Knowing what is a key detail versus extraneous information comes with experience; however, using an iterative process and revisiting your model helps to flesh out what needs to be there. As UML moves closer to tool automation with practices like MDA and Software Factories, the models often become more and more detailed and therefore complete. The difference is the tool support that helps vary the level of abstraction depending on your needs.

UML is designed to be open to interpretation. While the UML specification does a good job of laying down the groundwork for a modeling language, it is critical that within an organization or group of users you establish how and when to use a language feature. For example, some organizations use an aggregation relationship to indicate a C++ pointer and a composition relationship to indicate a C++ reference. There is nothing inherently wrong with this distinction, but it's something that isn't going to be immediately obvious to someone not familiar with that organization's modeling technique. It is a good practice to put together a document on modeling guidelines; it helps novice users get up to speed quicker and helps experienced users really think about how they represent something and consider a potentially better notation.

UML is intended to be extended. UML includes several mechanisms to allow customization and refinement of the language. Such mechanisms as adornments, constraints, and stereotypes provide ways to capture specific details that aren't easily expressed using classifiers and relationships. Typically these are grouped into what are known as UML *profiles*. For example, you can put together a Java 2 Enterprise Edition (J2EE) profile that includes stereotypes for sessionbean or javadataobject. If you are modeling a complex domain, consider putting together a UML profile that lets you easily identify elements as concepts in your domain, such as mutualfund or securitymonitor.

2

Class Diagrams

Class diagrams are one of the most fundamental diagram types in UML. They are used to capture the static relationships of your software; in other words, how things are put together.

When writing software you are constantly making design decisions: what classes hold references to other classes, which class "owns" some other class, and so on. Class diagrams provide a way to capture this "physical" structure of a system.

Classes

A class represents a group of things that have common state and behavior. You can think of a class as a blueprint for an object in an object-oriented system. In UML speak, a class is a kind of *classifier*. For example, Volkswagen, Toyota, and Ford are all cars, so you can represent them using a class named Car. Each specific type of car is an *instance* of that class, or an *object*. A class may represent a tangible and concrete concept, such as an invoice; it may be abstract, such as a document or a vehicle (as opposed to an invoice, or a motorcycle greater than 1000 cc), or it may represent an intangible concept such as a high-risk investment strategy.

You represent a class with a rectangular box divided into *compartments*. A compartment is simply an area in the rectangle to write information. The first compartment holds the name of the class, the second holds attributes (see "Attributes"), and the third is used for operations (see "Operations"). You can hide any compartment of the class if that increases the readability of your diagram. When reading a diagram, you can make no assumptions about a missing compartment; it doesn't mean it is empty. You may add compartments to a class to show additional information, such as exceptions or events, though this is outside of the typical notation.

UML suggests that the class name:

- Start with a capital letter
- Be centered in the top compartment
- Be written in a boldface font
- Be written in italics if the class is *abstract* (see "Abstract Classes")

Figure 2-1 shows a simple class.

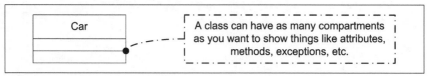

Figure 2-1. Simple class representation

Objects

An object is an *instance* of a class. For example, you may have several instances of a class named Car: one two-door red car, one four-door blue car, and one hatchback green car. Each instance of Car is an object and may be given its own name, though it is common to see unnamed, or anonymous, objects on object diagrams. Typically you show the name of the object followed by a colon followed by its type (i.e., class). You show that this is an instance of a class by underlining the name and type. Figure 2-2 shows an instance of a class Car named Toyota. Note that in this figure, we have hidden the empty compartments.

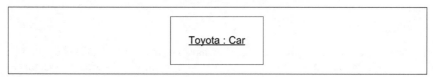

Figure 2-2. An instance of Car

Attributes

Details of a class (the color of a car, the number of sides in a shape, etc.) are represented as *attributes*. Attributes can be simple primitive types (integers, floating-point numbers, etc.) or relationships to other, complex objects (see "Relationships").

An attribute can be shown using two different notations: inlined or relationships between classes. In addition, notation is available to show such things as multiplicity, uniqueness, and ordering. This section introduces both notations, and then describes the details of the attribute specification.

Inlined Attributes

You can list a class's attributes right in rectangle notation; these are typically called *inlined attributes*. There is no semantic difference between inlined attributes and attributes by relationship; it's simply a matter of how much detail you want to present (or, in the case of primitives like integers, how much detail you *can* present).

To represent an attribute within the body of a class, place the attribute in the second compartment of the class. UML refers to inlined attributes as *attribute notation*. Inlined attributes use the following notation:

```
visibility / name : type multiplicity = default
   {property strings and constraints}

visibility ::= {+|-|#|~}

multiplicity ::= [lower..upper]
```

Figure 2-3 lists several attributes, demonstrating various aspects of attribute notation.

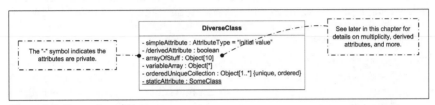

Figure 2-3. Example attributes

The syntax elements are:

visibility
Indicates the visibility of the attribute. Use the following symbols: +, -, #, or ~ for public, private, protected, or package, respectively (see "Visibility" in Chapter 3).

/
Indicates the attribute is *derived*. A derived attribute is simply one that can be computed from other attributes of the class. See "Derived Attributes."

name
Is a noun or short phrase naming the attribute. Typically the first letter is lowercase, and the first letter of each subsequent word is capitalized.

type
Is the type of the attribute as another classifier, typically a class, interface, or built-in type like *int*.

multiplicity
Specifies how many instances of the attribute's type are referenced by this attribute. Can be absent (meaning multiplicity of 1), a single integer, or a range of values specified between square brackets separated by "..". Use * as the upperbound to represent the upper limit or * on its own to mean zero or more. See "Multiplicity."

default
Is the default value of the attribute.

property strings
> Is a collection of properties, or tags, that can be attached to attributes. These are typically context-specific and denote such things as ordering or uniqueness. They are surrounded by {} and separated by commas. See "Properties."

constraints
> Are one or more restrictions placed on an attribute. They may be natural language or use a formal grammar such as the OCL. See "Constraints."

Attributes by Relationship

You may also represent attributes using the relationship notation. The relationship notation results in a larger class diagram, but it can provide greater detail for complex attribute types. The relationship notation also conveys exactly how the attribute is contained within a class (see "Relationships" for information on the types of relationships). For example, if you are modeling a Car, you can show that a car *contains* an Engine much more clearly using relationships than you can just by listing an attribute in the Car's rectangle. However, showing the Car's name by relationship is probably overkill because it is likely just a string.

To represent an attribute using relationships you use one of the association relationships between the class containing the attribute and the class that represents the attribute, as shown in Figure 2-4, which shows that the relationship between a car and its engine has a multiplicity of 1; a car has one engine.

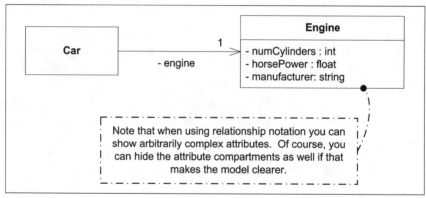

Figure 2-4. Attribute using relationship notation

Yes, yes, as my editor pointed out, some cars like the Toyota Prius have two engines. Work with me here.

Relationship notation supports the same syntax as inlined notation, though the layout is slightly different. The attribute's visibility and name are placed near the relationship line. Don't use square brackets for multiplicity, but do place the multiplicity specification near the attribute's classifier.

Like multiplicity, you can place constraints on attributes (see "Constraints"). In relationship notation, you write constraints near the attribute's classifier along the relationship line. UML allows relationship notation to also express constraints between attributes, as shown in Figure 2-5.

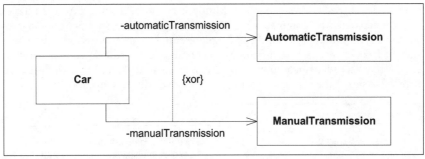

Figure 2-5. Relationship notation using constraints

In Figure 2-5, the standard UML constraint xor shows that only automaticTransmission or manualTransmission can be set at any given time (exclusive or). You need to express this constraint in a note if the inlined attribute notation was used.

Derived Attributes

The derived notation, which is the leading forward slash (/), can be used as an indicator to the implementer that the attribute may not be strictly necessary. For example, let's say you modeled a bank account with a simple class named Account. This class stores the current balance as a floating-point number named balance. To keep track of whether this account is overdrawn, you add a boolean named overdrawn. Whether the account is overdrawn is really based on whether the balance is positive, not the boolean you added. You can indicate this to the developer by showing that overdrawn is a derived attribute, with its state based on balance. Figure 2-6 shows how balance and overdrawn can be represented using a note to convey the relationship.

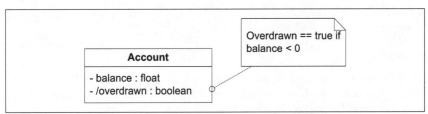

Figure 2-6. Derived attribute

The UML specification notes that a derived attribute is typically readOnly, meaning a user may not modify the value. However, if a user is permitted to modify the value, the class is expected to update the source of the derived information appropriately.

Attribute Multiplicity

The multiplicity of an attribute specifies how many instances of the attribute's type are created when the owning class is instantiated. For example, our Car class will likely have four wheels, so the multiplicity of the wheel attribute is 4. If no multiplicity is specified, 1 is implied. Multiplicity can be a single integer, a list of integers separated by commas, or a range of values. When specifying a range of values, an infinite upper bound can be represented as an *; if no lower bound is specified, an * means zero or more. The multiplicity value is shown between square brackets as a single integer or as two integers separated by two dots (..). Figure 2-7 shows the various ways to represent an attribute's multiplicity.

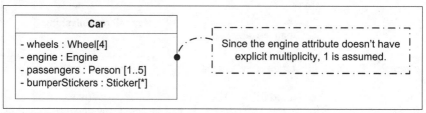

Figure 2-7. Multiplicity examples

Ordering

An attribute with a multiplicity greater than 1 can be specified to be *ordered*. If the attribute is ordered, the elements must be stored sequentially. For example, you can specify that a list of names be stored alphabetically by marking the list as ordered. Exactly what it means for attributes to be stored sequentially typically depends on the attribute type. By default, attributes are *not* ordered. To mark an attribute as ordered, specify the property ordered after the attribute in braces, as shown in Figure 2-8.

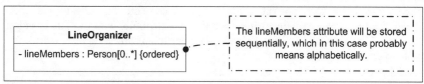

Figure 2-8. Ordered multiplicity

Uniqueness

In addition to being ordered, an attribute with multiplicity greater than 1 may be required to be *unique*. If an attribute is required to be unique, each element of this attribute must be unique. By default, attributes with multiplicity greater than 1 *are unique*, meaning there can be no duplicates in the elements this attribute holds. For example, if a class held a list of voters and each person was allowed to vote only once, each element in the list would be unique. To make an attribute unique, place the keyword unique after the attribute in braces, as shown in Figure 2-9. To allow an attribute to hold duplicates of an object, simply use the property not unique.

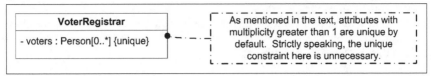

VoterRegistrar
- voters : Person[0..*] {unique}

As mentioned in the text, attributes with multiplicity greater than 1 are unique by default. Strictly speaking, the unique constraint here is unnecessary.

Figure 2-9. Unique multiplicity

Collection types

The UML specification specifies a set of mappings from the various ordered and uniqueness properties to UML collection types. Table 2-1 shows the mappings from attribute properties to the UML collection type. Note that the collection types shown in Table 2-1 are UML mappings and may not map directly to classes in a target language.

Table 2-1. Collection types for attributes

Order	Uniqueness	Associated collection type
False	False	Bag
True	True	OrderedSet
False	True	Set
True	False	Sequence

For example, to show that a bank's clients should be represented using an OrderedSet, you can model the clients attribute as shown in Figure 2-10.

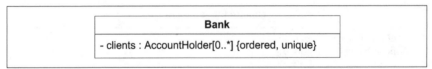

Bank
- clients : AccountHolder[0..*] {ordered, unique}

Figure 2-10. Example attribute stored in an OrderedSet

Attribute Properties

In addition to the properties associated with multiplicity, an attribute may have a number of properties set to convey additional information to the reader of the diagram. The common properties defined by UML are:

readOnly
> Specifies that the attribute may not be modified once the initial value is set. This typically maps to a *constant* in a development language. UML doesn't specify when the initial value must be set, though if you specify the default value for an attribute it is considered the initial value and may not be changed.

union
> Specifies that the attribute type is a union of the possible values for this attribute. Frequently this is used with the derived property to indicate that an attribute is a derived union of another set of attributes.

subsets <attribute-name>

Specifies that this attribute type is a subset of all the valid values for the given attribute. This isn't a common property, but if used, it is typically associated with subclasses of an attribute type.

redefines <attribute-name>

Specifies that this attribute acts as an alias for the given attribute. Though uncommon, this attribute can be used to show that a subclass has an attribute that is an alias for a superclass's attribute.

composite

Specifies that this attribute is part of a whole-part relationship with the classifier. See "Relationships" for more information on composition.

Constraints

Constraints represent restrictions placed on an element. They may be natural language or use a formal grammar such as the OCL; however, they must evaluate to a boolean expression. You typically show constraints between curly braces ({}) after the element they restrict, though they may be placed in a note and linked to the element using a dashed line.

You can name a constraint by specifying the name followed by a colon (:) before the boolean expression. This is frequently used to identify constraints on an operation (see "Operation Constraints").

Figure 2-11 shows several constraints on attributes and operations.

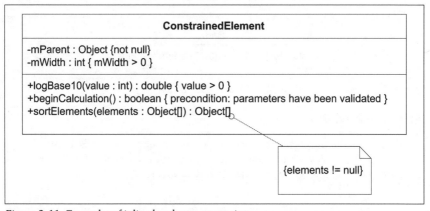

Figure 2-11. Examples of inlined and note constraints

Static Attributes

Static attributes are attributes of the class rather than of an instance of the class. For example, you can initialize constant values for a class and share them between all instances of the class. You represent static attributes by underlining their specification in both inlined and relationship-based presentations, as shown in Figure 2-12.

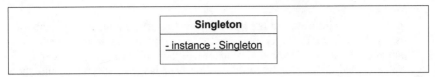

Figure 2-12. Static attribute

Operations

Operations are features of classes that specify how to invoke a particular behavior. For example, a class may offer an operation to draw a rectangle on the screen or count the number of items selected in a list. UML makes a clear distinction between the specification of how to invoke a behavior (an operation) and the actual implementation of that behavior (a method). See "Methods" for more information.

You place operations in a separate compartment with the following syntax:

    visibility name (parameters) : return-type {properties}

where parameters are written as:

    direction parameter_name : type [multiplicity]
      = default_value { properties }

Figure 2-13 shows several example operations on a class.

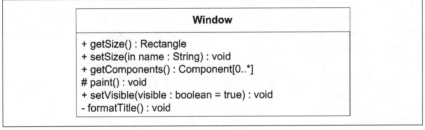

Figure 2-13. Example operations on a class

The syntax elements are:

visibility
Indicates the visibility of the operation. Use the following symbols: +, -, #, or ~ for public, private, protected, or package, respectively (see "Visibility" in Chapter 3).

name
Is a short phrase naming the operation. Operations are usually verb phrases representing actions the classifier should perform on behalf of the caller. The UML specification recommends that the first letter of an operation be lower-case, with all of the following words starting with a capital letter and running together. See Figure 2-13 for an example.

return-type

Is the type of information the operation will return, if any. If no information is returned from the operation (called a subroutine in some development languages), the return type should be void. If the operation does return a value (called a function in some development languages), you should show the type of the returned value, such as another classifier, a primitive type, or a collection. The UML specification states that the return type is optional. If it's left off, you can't assume anything about the return value of the operation, or even if one exists.

properties

Specifies constraints and properties associated with an operation. These are optional; if you don't use properties you don't show the curly braces. See "Operation Constraints" for more information.

Parameter syntax elements are:

direction

An optional part of the syntax that indicates how a parameter is used by an operation. It is one of in, inout, out, or return. in states that the parameter is passed to the operation by the caller. inout states that the parameter is passed by the caller and is then possibly modified by the operation and passed back out. out states that the parameter isn't set by the caller but is modified by the operation and is passed back out. return indicates that the value set by the caller is passed back out as a return value.

parameter_name

Is a noun or noun phrase naming the parameter. Typically the parameter name starts with a lowercase letter, with any subsequent words starting with a capital letter.

type

Is the type of the parameter. This is typically another class, interface, collection, or primitive type.

multiplicity

Specifies how many instances of the parameter's type are present. Can be absent (meaning multiplicity of 1), a single integer, a list of integers separated by commas, or a range of values specified between square brackets separated by "..". An infinite upper bound can be represented as an *; if no lower bound specified, an * means zero or more. See "Multiplicity."

default_value

Specifies the default value of this parameter. The default value is optional. If it isn't present, you don't show the equals sign. Note that UML doesn't specify if a parameter with a default value may be left out when invoking an operation (e.g., C++'s default parameter value implementation). The actual syntax for invoking an operation is language-dependent.

properties

Specifies any parameter-related properties and is specified between curly braces. These are typically defined within the context of a specific model, with a few exceptions: ordered, readOnly, and unique. See "Multiplicity" and

"Properties" for more information. Properties are optional for parameters; if they aren't used, don't show the curly braces.

Operation Constraints

An operation may have several constraints associated with it that help define how the operation interacts with the rest of the system. Together, constraints on an operation establish a contract that an implementation of the operation must obey.

Constraints on an operation follow the usual constraint notation and are placed either immediately after the operation signature or in a note attached with a dashed line. See "Constraints" for more information.

Preconditions

Preconditions capture what the state of the system must be before an operation can be invoked. Practically speaking, you really can't express the state of the *entire* system. Instead, preconditions typically express the valid values for parameters, the state of the class owning the operation, or a few key attributes of the system.

The specification explicitly states that the operation doesn't need to check the preconditions in the body of the operation before executing; theoretically the operation will not even be invoked if the preconditions aren't met. In practice, few languages offer such protection. If someone took the time to express them, it is usually in your best interest to verify the preconditions are correct when implementing an operation.

As a developer, preconditions offer you one of the few chances to "cover your butt" and say exactly how you expect things to be when your implementation is invoked; use them.

Figure 2-14 shows several examples of preconditions.

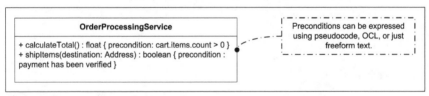

Figure 2-14. Preconditions for operations

Postconditions

Postconditions capture guarantees about the state of the system after an operation has executed. Like preconditions, postconditions typically express the state of one or more key attributes of the system, or some guarantee about the state of the class owning the operation.

Figure 2-15 shows example postconditions linked to an operation.

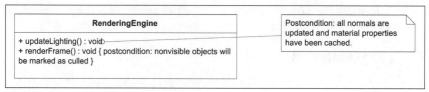

Figure 2-15. Postconditions for operations

Body conditions

An operation may have a bodyCondition that constrains the return value. The bodyCondition is separate from the postcondition because the bodyCondition may be replaced by methods of subclasses of the owning class. (See "Generalization" for more information on subclasses.) For example, a class named Window may specify a body condition for a method named getSize() that requires the length and width of a window be nonzero. A subclass named SquareWindow may provide its own body condition stating that the width must equal the height. The bodyCondition is similar to the pre- and postconditions in that the constraint may be expressed in natural language or in OCL. See "Constraints" for more information. Figure 2-16 shows an example of a bodyCondition on an operation.

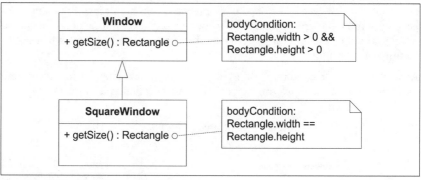

Figure 2-16. Body conditions for operations

Query operations

An operation may be declared as a *query* operation if the implementation of the operation doesn't modify the owning class in any way. In practice, modelers often use the query property to indicate a method that doesn't change any meaningful attribute of an object. For example, there may be internal cache attributes that are updated as a result of a query. The important thing is that the state of the system, from an external perspective, isn't changed by the query method; there can be no side effects to calling the method.

You indicate a query method by placing the query constraint after the operation signature. For example, an operation named getAge() that simply returns an integer without changing any internal value of the owning class would be considered a query method. In C++, this typically maps to a const method. Figure 2-17 shows several query methods on a class.

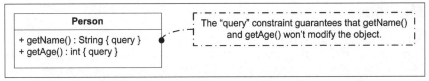

Figure 2-17. Example query operations

Exceptions

While they're technically not constraints, you may express exceptions thrown by an operation using similar notation. Exceptions are typically other classes (often stereotyped with the keyword «exception», though this is simply by convention) that are thrown by an operation in the event of an error. You can list thrown exceptions in a note attached to an operation using a dashed line. Figure 2-18 shows an example of an operation that throws several exceptions.

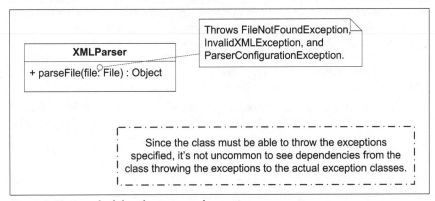

Figure 2-18. A method that throws several exceptions

Static Operations

Operations typically specify behavior for an *instance* of a class. However, UML allows for an operation to specify behavior for the *class itself*. These operations are called *static operations* and are invoked directly on the class, not on an instance. Static operations are frequently used as utility operations that don't need to use the attributes of the owning class. UML doesn't formally discuss the notation of these operations, but it is typical to see them represented with the same convention as static attributes. You indicate an operation is static by underlining the operation signature. Figure 2-19 shows an example of a static operation.

Figure 2-19. A class with a static operation

Methods

A *method* is an implementation of an operation. Each class typically provides an implementation for its operations or inherits them from its superclass (see "Generalization"). If a class doesn't provide an implementation for an operation, and one isn't provided by its superclass, the operation is considered *abstract*. See "Abstract Classes" for more information. Because methods are implementations of operations, there is no notation for a method; simply show an operation on a class.

Abstract Classes

An *abstract class* is typically a class that provides an operation signature, but no implementation; however, you can have an abstract class that has no operations at all. An abstract class is useful for identifying common functionality across several types of objects. For example, you can have an abstract class named Movable. A Movable object has a current position and the ability to move somewhere else using an operation named move( ). There can be several specializations of this abstract class—a Car, a Grasshopper, and a Person, each of which provides a different implementation of move( ). Because the base class Movable doesn't have an implementation for move( ), the class is said to be abstract.

You show a class is abstract by writing its name in italics. Show each abstract operation in italics as well. Figure 2-20 is an example of the abstract class Movable.

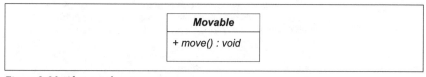

Figure 2-20. Abstract class

An abstract class can't be instantiated; it must be subclassed and then a subclass which does provide the operation implementation can be instantiated. See "Relationships" for more information on subclasses.

Relationships

Classes in isolation would not provide much insight into how a system is designed. UML provides several ways of representing relationships between classes. Each of UML relationship represents a different type of connection between classes and has subtleties that aren't fully captured in the UML specification. When modeling in the real world, be sure that your intended viewers understand what you are conveying with your various relationships. We say this both as a warning to the modeler and as a slight disclaimer that the following explanations are our interpretation of the UML specification. For example, the debate over when to use aggregation versus composition is ongoing. To help determine which relationship is most appropriate, we offer a short phrase for each type that may help make the distinction. Again, the important thing is to be consistent within your model.

Dependency

The weakest relationship between classes is a *dependency* relationship. Dependency between classes means that one class uses, or has knowledge of, another class. It is typically a transient relationship, meaning a dependent class briefly interacts with the target class but typically doesn't retain a relationship with it for any real length of time.

Dependencies are typically read as "...uses a...". For example, if you have a class named Window that sends out a class named WindowClosingEvent when it is about to be closed, you would say "Window uses a WindowClosingEvent."

You show a dependency between classes using a dashed line with an arrow pointing from the dependent class to the class that is used. Figure 2-21 shows a dependency between a class named Window and a class named WindowClosingEvent.

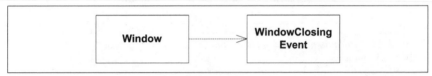

Figure 2-21. Window's dependency on WindowClosingEvent

You can likely assume from Figure 2-21 that Window doesn't retain a relationship with a WindowClosingEvent for any real length of time. It simply uses them when needed and then forgets about them.

Association

Associations are stronger than dependencies and typically indicate that one class retains a relationship to another class over an extended period of time. The lifelines of two objects linked by associations are probably not tied together (meaning one can be destroyed without necessarily destroying the other).

Associations are typically read as "...has a...". For example, if you have a class named Window that has a reference to the current mouse cursor, you would say "Window has a Cursor". Note that there is a fine line between "...has a..." and "...owns a..." (see "Aggregation" later in this section). In this case, Window doesn't own the Cursor; Cursor is shared between all applications in the system. However, Window has a reference to it so that the Window can hide it, change its shape, etc. You show an association using a solid line between the classes participating in the relationship. Figure 2-22 shows an association between Window and Cursor.

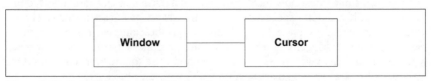

Figure 2-22. Association showing Window "has a" Cursor

Navigability

Associations have explicit notation to express navigability. If you can navigate from one class to another, you show an arrow in the direction of the class you can navigate to. If you can navigate in both directions, it is common practice to not show any arrows at all, but as the UML specification points out, if you suppress all arrows you can't distinguish nonnavigable associations from two-way associations. However, it is extremely rare to use a nonnavigable association in the real world, so this is unlikely to be a problem.

You can explicitly forbid navigation from one class to another by placing a small X on the association line at the end of the class you can't navigate to. Figure 2-23 shows an association between a class named Window and a class named Cursor. Because you can't navigate from an instance of Cursor to an instance of Window, we explicitly show the navigability arrow and an X where appropriate.

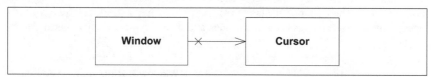

Figure 2-23. Association between Window and Cursor showing you can't navigate from Cursor to Window

Naming an association

Associations may be adorned with several symbols to add information to your model. The simplest is a solid arrowhead showing the direction in which the viewer should read the association. It is common to include a short phrase along with the arrowhead to provide some context for the association. The phrase used with the association doesn't typically generate into any form of code representation; it is purely for modeling purposes. Figure 2-24 shows the solid arrowhead on the Window to Cursor association.

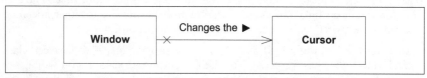

Figure 2-24. Shows how to read the association between Window and Cursor

Multiplicity

Because associations typically represent lasting relationships, they are often used to indicate attributes of a class. As mentioned in the "Attributes by Relationship" section, you can express how many instances of a particular class are involved in a relationship. If you don't specify a value, a multiplicity of 1 is assumed. To show a different value, simply place the multiplicity specification near the owned class. See "Attribute Multiplicity" for the allowable multiplicity types. Note that when you use multiplicity with an association, you don't use square brackets around the values. Figure 2-25 shows an association with explicit multiplicity.

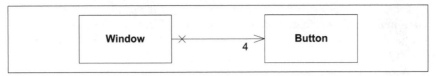

Figure 2-25. A simple association showing four Buttons in a Window

The properties related to multiplicity may be applied to associations as well. See "Properties" for the names and definitions of allowed properties.

Aggregation

Aggregation is a stronger version of association. Unlike association, aggregation typically implies ownership and may imply a relationship between lifelines. Aggregations are usually read as "...owns a...". For example, if you had a classed named Window that stored its position and size in a Rectangle class, you would say the "Window owns a Rectangle." The rectangle may be shared with other classes, but the Window has an intimate relationship with the Rectangle. This is subtly different from a basic association; it has a stronger connotation. However, it's not the strongest relationship you can have between classes. If the relationship is more of a whole part (class A "...is part of..." class B), you should look at *composition*.

You show an aggregation with a diamond shape next to the owning class and a solid line pointing to the owned class. Figure 2-26 shows an example aggregation between a class named Window and a class named Rectangle.

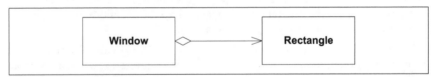

Figure 2-26. Window "owns a" Rectangle

As with the association relationship, you can show navigability and multiplicity on an aggregation line. See "Association" for examples.

Composition

Composition represents a very strong relationship between classes, to the point of containment. Composition is used to capture a whole-part relationship. The "part" piece of the relationship can be involved in only one composition relationship at any given time. The lifetime of instances involved in composition relationships is almost always linked; if the larger, owning instance is destroyed, it almost always destroys the part piece. UML does allow the part to be associated with a different owner before destruction, thus preserving its existence, but this is typically an exception rather than the rule.

A composition relationship is usually read as "...is part of...", which means you need to read the composition from the part to the whole. For example, if you say that a window in your system *must* have a titlebar, you can represent this with a class named Titlebar that "...is part of..." a class named Window.

You show a composition relationship using a filled diamond next to the owning class and a solid line pointing to the owned class. Figure 2-27 shows an example composition relationship between a class named Window and a class named Titlebar.

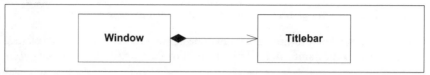

Figure 2-27. Titlebar "is a part of" Window

As with the association relationship, you can show navigability and multiplicity on a composition line. See "Association" for examples.

Generalization

A *generalization* relationship conveys that the target of the relationship is a general, or less specific, version of the source class or interface. Generalization relationships are often used to pull out commonality between difference classifiers. For example, if you had a class named Cat and a class named Dog, you can create a generalization of both of those classes called Animal. A full discussion of how and when to use generalization (especially versus interface realization) is the subject for an object-oriented analysis and design book and isn't covered here.

Generalizations are usually read as "...is a...", starting from the more specific class and reading toward the general class. Going back to the Cat and Dog example, you would say "a Cat...is a...Animal" (grammar aside).

You show a generalization relationship with a solid line with a closed arrow, pointing from the specific class to the general class. Figure 2-28 shows an example of the Cat to Animal relationship.

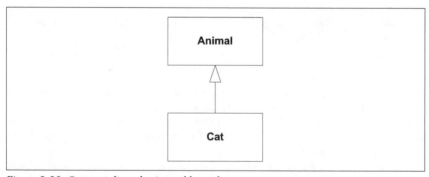

Figure 2-28. Cat specializes the Animal base class

Unlike associations, generalization relationships are typically not named and don't have any kind of multiplicity. UML allows for multiple inheritance, meaning a class can have more than one generalization with each representing an aspect of the decedent class. However, some modern languages (e.g., Java and

C#) don't support multiple inheritance; interfaces and interface realization are used instead.

Association Classes

Often the relationship between two elements isn't a simple structural connection. For example, a football player may be associated with a league by virtue of being on a team. If the association between two elements is complex, you can represent the connection using an *association class*. An association class is an association that has a name and attributes, like a normal class. You show an association class like a regular class with a dashed line connecting it to the association it represents. Figure 2-29 shows a football player's relationships to a league.

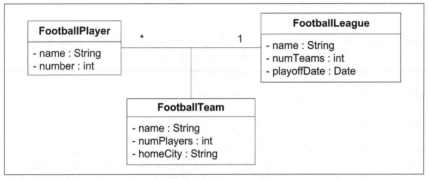

Figure 2-29. Example association class

When translated into code, relationships with association classes often result in three classes: one for each end of the association and one for the association class itself. There may or may not be a direct link between the association ends; the implementation may require you to traverse through the association class to get to the opposite end of the link. In other words, FootballPlayer may not have a direct reference to FootballLeague but may have a reference to FootballTeam instead. FootballTeam would then have a reference to FootballLeague. How the relationships are constructed is a matter of implementation choices; however, the fundamental concept of an association class is unchanged.

Association Qualifiers

Relationships between elements are often keyed, or indexed, by some other value. For example, a bank patron may be identified by her account number, or a tax payer by his Social Security number. UML provides association *qualifiers* to capture such information. A qualifier is typically an attribute of the target element, though this isn't required. You show a qualifier by placing a small rectangle between the association and the source element. Draw the name of the qualifier (usually the name of an attribute) in the rectangle. Figure 2-30 shows the relationship between the IRS and a taxpayer qualified by the taxpayer's Social Security number.

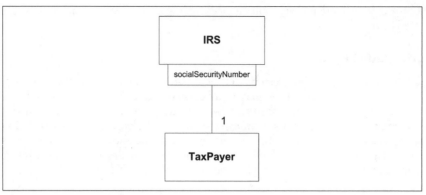

Figure 2-30. An association qualifier

Notice that the multiplicity between the association qualifier and TaxPayer is 1. Obviously the IRS is associated with more than one TaxPayer, but by using qualifiers, you indicate that a socialSecurityNumber uniquely identifies a single TaxPayer within the IRS.

Interfaces

An *interface* is a classifier that has declarations of properties and methods but no implementations. You can use interfaces to group common elements between classifiers and provide a contract a classifier that provides an implementation of an interface must obey. For example, you can create an interface named Sortable that has one operation named comesBefore(...). Any class that realizes the Sortable interface must provide an implementation of comesBefore(...).

Some modern languages, such as C++, don't support the concept of interfaces; UML interfaces are typically represented as pure abstract classes. Other languages, such as Java, do support interfaces but don't allow them to have properties. The moral is that you should be aware of how your model is going to be implemented when modeling your system.

There are two representations for an interface; which one you should use depends on what you're trying to show. The first representation is the standard UML classifier notation with the stereotype «interface». Figure 2-31 shows the Sortable interface.

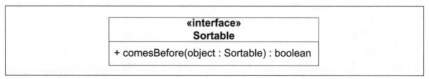

Figure 2-31. The Sortable interface

The second representation of an interface is the ball-and-socket notation. This representation shows less detail for the interface but is more convenient for showing relationships to classes. The interface is simply shown as a ball with the name of the interface written below it. Classes dependent on this interface are shown attached to a socket matching the interface. Figure 2-32 shows the Sortable interface using the ball-and-socket notation.

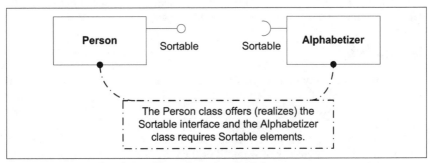

Figure 2-32. Examples of providing and requiring interfaces

Because an interface specifies the contract only for a set of features, you can't instantiate an interface directly. Instead, a class is said to *realize* an interface if it provides an implementation for the operations and properties. You show realization using a dashed line starting at the realizing classifier and leading to the interface, with a closed arrowhead at the end. Classes that are dependent on the interface are shown using a dashed line with an open arrow (dependency). Figure 2-33 shows a class that realizes the Sortable interface and a class that is dependent on it.

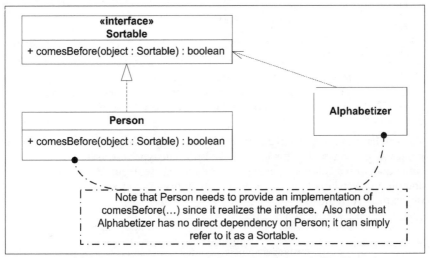

Figure 2-33. Person realizes the Sortable interface and Alphabetizer depends on it

Providing an implementation of an operation is straightforward. You must provide an implementation on a realizing classifier with the same signature as the operation on the interface. Typically there are semantic constraints associated with an operation that must be honored by any implementation. Realizing a property is more subtle. A property on an interface states that any class that realizes the interface must store the data specified by the property *in some way*. A property on an interface doesn't necessarily mean there will be an associated property on a realizing classifier. However, the classifier must be able to store the data represented by the property and provide a means to manipulate it.

Templates

Just as interfaces allow you to provide specifications for *objects* your class will interact with, UML allows you to provide abstractions for the type of *class* your class may interact with. For example, you can write a List class that can hold any type of object (in C++ this would probably be a void*, in Java and C# it would probably be an Object). However, while you wanted your List class to be able to support any type of object, you want all of the objects in a given list to be of the same type. UML allows you to create and specify these kinds of abstractions using *templates*.

You can indicate that a class is a templated (also called *parameterized*) class by drawing a dashed rectangle in the upper-right corner of the class. For each element you would like to template, you need to specify a name to act as a placeholder for the actual type. Write the placeholder name in the rectangle. Figure 2-34 shows an example of a List class that can support any type.

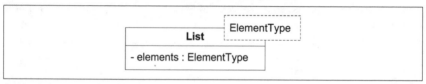

Figure 2-34. A templated List class

 This example uses ElementType as the name of the templated type for clarity. In practice, this is often abbreviated to just T.

You can have multiple templated types within a single class; just separate the type names with a comma (,). If you need to restrict the types the user may substitute, show that with a colon (:) followed by the type name. Figure 2-35 shows a more complicated version of the List class that requires a Sorter along with the type of object to store in the list.

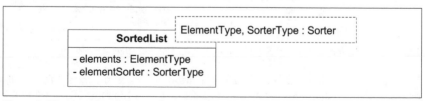

Figure 2-35. A templated class with type restrictions

Specifying restrictions on a type that may be used is functionally similar to specifying an interface for a templated member, except that the user may be able to further restrict an instance of your class by specifying a subclass of your type.

When a user creates an instance of a List, she needs to specify the actual type to use in place of ElementType. This is called *binding* a type to a template. You show binding with the keyword «bind», followed by a type specification using the following syntax:

```
< TemplatedType -> RealType >
```

You can use the binding syntax whenever you refer to a templated class to indicate you want to use a bound version of that class. This is called *explicit binding*. For example, Figure 2-36 shows a subclass of List called EmployeeList that binds the ElementType of List to a class named Employee.

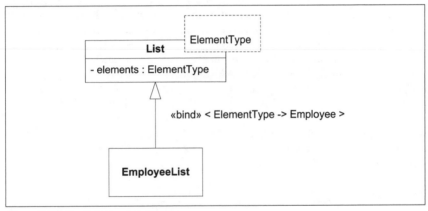

Figure 2-36. Explicit template binding

The bind keyword also indicates what types should be used with an instance of a template. This is called *implicit binding* and is shown in Figure 2-37.

ExampleList : List <ElementType->Employee>

Figure 2-37. Implicit template binding

Variations on Class Diagrams

Because class diagrams model structures well, they can be used to capture well-defined, hierarchical information. Class diagrams have been used to capture XML and database schemas with some degree of success. In the interest of full disclosure, people who deal with XML and database schemas extensively have reservations about using class diagrams to capture the information, specifically because class diagrams are so generic. Each domain has its own notation that may be better suited to capturing complex relationships or domain-specific information. However, UML has the benefit of being a common language that is understood by those outside the XML and database domains.

XML Schemas

The structural design of an XML document can be captured in an XML schema. XML schemas are to XML documents as classes are to objects; XML documents are instances of a schema. Therefore, it's not a giant leap to realize that class diagrams can be used to model XML schemas. XML schemas are described using the XML Structure Definition Language (XSDL). XSDL is a text language (as opposed to the graphical nature of UML) and can be verbose; mapping XSDL to UML can make it much easier to digest a schema document.

The fundamental elements of XSDL are XML elements, which are connected in sequences, choices, and complex structures. Each element may have extra information attached to it using (conveniently enough) attributes. Modelers typically represent XML elements as classes and XSDL attributes as UML attributes. Each element is linked to the next using composition arrows. Multiplicity specifications on the relationships show how many times one element appears within another. Example 2-1 is a sample XML document that describes a piece of equipment.

Example 2-1. A sample XML document

```
<?xml version="1.0" encoding="UTF-8"?>
<equipmentlist xmlns:xsi="http://www.w3.org/2001/XMLSchema-instance"
xsi:noNamespaceSchemaLocation="equipment.xsd">
    <equipment equipmentid="H-1">
        <shortname>
            <langstring lang="en">Hammer</langstring>
        </shortname>
        <technicalcontact>
            <contact>
                <name>Ron</name>
                <telephone>555-1212</telephone>
            </contact>
        </technicalcontact>
        <trainingcontact>
            <contact>
                <name>Joe</name>
                <email>joe@home.com</email>
            </contact>
        </trainingcontact>
    </equipment>
</equipmentlist>
```

Example 2-2 is the XSDL that describes the XML document.

Example 2-2. XML schema describing Example 2-1

```
<?xml version="1.0" encoding="ISO-8859-1"?>
<xs:schema xmlns:xs="http://www.w3.org/2001/XMLSchema"
elementFormDefault="qualified">
```

Example 2-2. XML schema describing Example 2-1 (continued)

```
<!-- ~Class: contact ~~~~~~~~~~~~~~~~~~~~~~~~~~~~~~~~~~~~ -->
<xs:element name="contact" type="contact"/>
<xs:complexType name="contact">
    <xs:sequence>
      <xs:element name="name" type="xs:string"/>
      <xs:choice>
        <xs:element name="telephone" type="xs:string"/>
        <xs:element name="email" type="xs:string"/>
      </xs:choice>
    </xs:sequence>
</xs:complexType>

<!-- ~Class: equipment ~~~~~~~~~~~~~~~~~~~~~~~~~~~~~~~~~~ -->
<xs:element name="equipment" type="equipment"/>
<xs:complexType name="equipment">
    <xs:sequence>
      <xs:element ref="shortname"/>
      <xs:element name="technicalcontact" type="technicalcontact"/>
      <xs:element name="trainingcontact" type="trainingcontact"/>
    </xs:sequence>
    <xs:attribute name="equipmentid" type="xs:string" use="required"/>
</xs:complexType>

<!-- ~Class: equipmentlist ~~~~~~~~~~~~~~~~~~~~~~~~~~~~~ -->
<xs:element name="equipmentlist" type="equipmentlist"/>
<xs:complexType name="equipmentlist">
    <xs:sequence>
      <xs:element ref="equipment" minOccurs="1" maxOccurs="unbounded"/>
    </xs:sequence>
</xs:complexType>

<!-- ~Class: <<XSDtopLevelAttribute>> lang~~~~~~~~~~~~ -->
<xs:attribute name="lang" type="xs:language"/>

<!-- ~Class: langstring ~~~~~~~~~~~~~~~~~~~~~~~~~~~~~~~~~ -->
<xs:element name="langstring" type="langstring"/>
<xs:complexType name="langstring">
    <xs:simpleContent>
      <xs:extension base="xs:string">
          <xs:attribute name="lang" use="required">
            <xs:simpleType>
                <xs:restriction base="xs:NMTOKEN">
                    <xs:enumeration value="en"/>
                    <xs:enumeration value="fr"/>
                </xs:restriction>
            </xs:simpleType>
          </xs:attribute>
      </xs:extension>
    </xs:simpleContent>
</xs:complexType>
```

Example 2-2. XML schema describing Example 2-1 (continued)

```
<!-- ~Class: shortname ~~~~~~~~~~~~~~~~~~~~~~~~~~~~~~~~~~~ -->
<xs:element name="shortname" type="shortname"/>
<xs:complexType name="shortname">
   <xs:sequence>
      <xs:element ref="langstring" minOccurs="1" maxOccurs="unbounded"/>
   </xs:sequence>
</xs:complexType>

<!-- ~Class: technicalcontact ~~~~~~~~~~~~~~~~~~~~~~~~~~ -->
<xs:element name="technicalcontact" type="technicalcontact"/>
<xs:complexType name="technicalcontact">
   <xs:sequence>
      <xs:element ref="contact" minOccurs="1" maxOccurs="unbounded"/>
   </xs:sequence>
</xs:complexType>

<!-- ~Class: trainingcontact ~~~~~~~~~~~~~~~~~~~~~~~~~~~ -->
<xs:element name="trainingcontact" type="trainingcontact"/>
<xs:complexType name="trainingcontact">
   <xs:sequence>
      <xs:element ref="contact" minOccurs="1" maxOccurs="unbounded"/>
   </xs:sequence>
</xs:complexType>
</xs:schema>
```

Figure 2-38 is a UML representation of the schema. Elements are represented as classes, with one exception: the contact definition includes a choice option. Figure 2-38 represents this using another class stereotyped as XSDchoice, and the options are represented as attributes of the class.

So, while UML simplifies a schema by representing the information graphically, details such as sequencing and type information can be lost without using a UML extension mechanism such as constraints or stereotypes.

Database Schemas

By mapping database tables to classes and table rows to attributes, you can capture a database schema fairly well using UML. Additional information such as primary keys, foreign keys, and constraints can be captured using UML constraints or stereotypes. You can show relationships between tables using associations between classes (usually composition relationships, but that is just by convention). Figure 2-39 shows a sample database schema represented using a UML class diagram.

As with XML schemas, few professional database administrators model databases using class diagrams. UML class diagrams are useful for conveying schema information in a common language, but they lack the expressive (and custom) capabilities of the more standard database notation, Entity Relation Diagrams (ERDs).

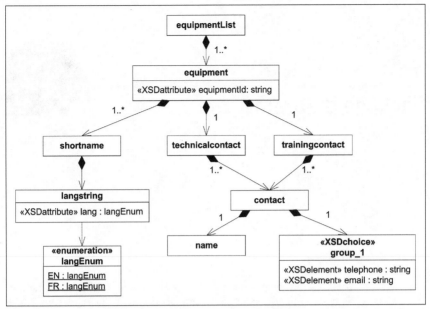

Figure 2-38. A class diagram representation of Example 2-2

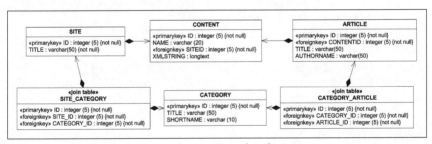

Figure 2-39. An example database schema using a class diagram

3

Package Diagrams

Packages provide a way to group related UML elements and scope their names. For example, you can put all elements having to do with 3D rendering into a package named 3DGraphics. Package diagrams provide a great way to visualize dependencies between parts of your system and are often used to look for problems or determine compilation order.

Nearly all UML elements can be grouped into packages, including packages themselves. Each package has a name that scopes each element in the package. For example, if you had a class named Timer in a package named Utilities, the fully qualified name for the class is Utilities::Timer. Elements in the same package can refer to each other without qualifying their names.

Representation

You show a package using a rectangle with a tab attached to the top left. Figure 3-1 shows the Utilities package.

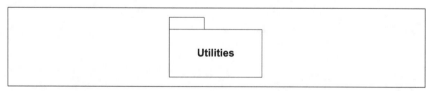

Figure 3-1. A simple package

You can show the elements contained within a package in two different ways. First, you can show the elements contained within the package by drawing them inside the large rectangle. If you use this representation, write the name of the package in the tab. Figure 3-2 shows the contents of the Utilities package inside of the package. To refer to the Timer class from outside of the Utilities package, you say Utilities::Timer.

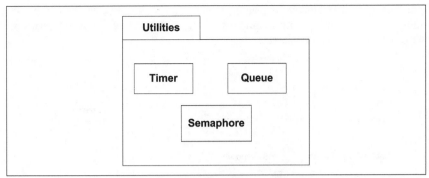

Figure 3-2. Several classes contained inside the Utilities package

The second representation uses a solid line pointing from the package to each contained element. You place a circle with a plus sign in it at the end nearest the package to indicate containment. If you use this representation, you should show the name of the package in the large rectangle rather than in the tab. This notation allows you to show more detail of the packaged elements. Figure 3-3 shows the same Utilities package but with the classes broken out.

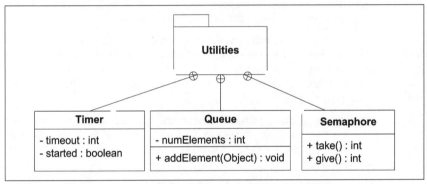

Figure 3-3. Elements owned by a package, shown outside of the package

You don't need to show all the elements contained within a package; if no elements are shown, no assumptions can be made about what the package contains.

Visibility

A package may specify visibility information for owned and imported elements, however elements may have only one of two levels of visibility: public or private. Public visibility means the element may be used outside the package (scoped by the package name). Private visibility means the element may be used only by other elements of the same package. Private visibility is useful for marking utility classes that help implement a subsystem or component you don't want to expose to the rest of the system.

You show public visibility by placing a plus sign before the element name. You show private visibility using a minus sign. Figure 3-4 shows the Utility package with some private helper classes.

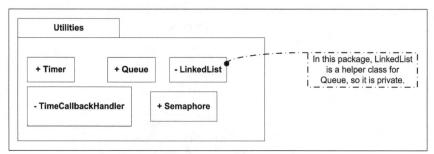

Figure 3-4. The Utilities package with public and private members

Importing and Accessing Packages

When accessing elements in one package from a different package, you must qualify the name of the element you are accessing. For example, if Car is a class in the Transportation package and you are trying to access it from a package named RoutePlanning, you need to qualify Car as Transportation::Car.

To simplify accessing elements in a different package, UML allows a package to *import* another package. Elements of the imported package are available without qualification in the importing package. So, if the RoutePlanning package imported the Transportation package, you can refer to Car without any qualifications from within the RoutePlanning package.

To show a package import, you draw a dashed line with an open arrow from the importing package to the imported package. Label this line with the «import» keyword. Figure 3-5 shows the RoutePlanning package importing the Transportation package.

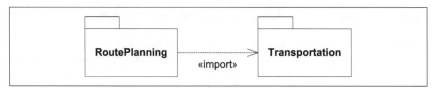

Figure 3-5. RoutePlanning importing the Transportation package

By default, imported elements are given public visibility in the importing package. UML allows you to specify that imported elements should be given private visibility, meaning they can't be used by anyone outside the importing package (including any packages that may import that package). To specify that imported elements should have private visibility, you use the «access» keyword rather than the «import» keyword. Figure 3-6 shows the RoutePlanning package importing the Transportation package and accessing the Algorithms package. If a package imports the `RoutePlanning` package, both packages can use public elements from `Transportation`, but they can't use anything in `Algorithms`.

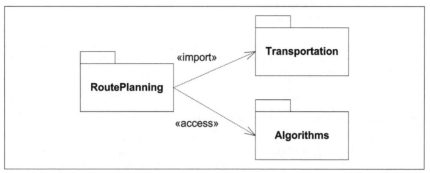

Figure 3-6. RoutePlanning importing the Transportation package but accessing only the Algorithms package

What package import and access actually mean in implementation can vary dramatically depending on your target language. For example, C# and Java have an explicit concept of packages and importing elements from packages. Java developers often import the `java.util` package into their program so they can reference the Java `Vector` class without qualifying it. However, C++ has a somewhat subtler concept of packages, called namespaces. How packages map to an implementation language is often up to the implementer.

Merging Packages

UML supports a somewhat complex concept of merging packages. Merging packages differs from importing packages in that *merge,* by definition, creates relationships between classes of the same name. The motivation behind package merging comes directly from the evolution of UML from 1.x to 2.0. UML 2.0 defines the base concept of elements and allows specific diagram types to extend a base concept without needing to provide a new name for it. For example, UML extends several core Behavioral State Machine concepts into Protocol State Machine concepts while retaining their original name.

When a package merges another package, any class of the same type and name automatically extends (or has a generalization relationship to) the original class. For example, UML can define the concept of the `include` relationship at a generic level and then specialize it for use cases inclusion and retain the name `include`. This type of extension has simplified the internals of the UML model but rarely makes an appearance in real-world development.

You show package merging using a dashed line with an open arrow from the merging package to the merged package. Label this line with the keyword «merge». Figure 3-7 shows an example of merging two packages.

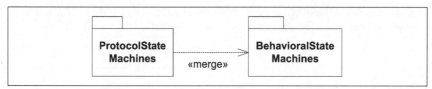

Figure 3-7. ProtocolStateMachines merging the elements from BehavioralStateMachines so it can add to the contained classes

The rules for package merge are:

- Private members of a package aren't merged with anything.
- Classes in the package performing the merge that have the same name and type as classes in the merged package(s) get a generalization relationship to the merged class(es). Note that this can result in multiple inheritance, but UML allows this.
- You can still reference any of the original classes by explicitly scoping the class using the original package name.
- Classes that exist only in the merged package or the merging package remain unchanged and are added to the merging package.
- Subpackages within the merged package are added to the merging package if they don't already exist.
- If a subpackage with the same name already exists in the merging package, another merge is started between the two subpackages.
- Any package imports from the merged package become package imports from the merging package. Elements that are imported aren't merged (i.e., aren't given generalization relationships). If an imported element conflicts with an element in the merging package, the merging package's element takes precedence and the imported element must be explicitly qualified.

Variations on Package Diagrams

This section presents two applications of class package diagrams and one application of use case packages. Although layering and simplification always motivate packaging, the term "simplification" means different things to different people. Simplification can mean:

- Easier to build and test
- Better tracking and project transparency
- Working at a stable overview without the noise of low-level churn
- Less conflict between distributed teams
- Easy refactoring and extension

Simplification likely means more apparent complexity to some constituency. Unless your packaging balances these diverse needs, you are likely to receive complaints of unnecessary complexity, no matter how noble your motives are.

Structuring a Project with Package Diagrams

Class packages organize a logical system during construction. They provide the terms for management and external stakeholders, as well as structure to contain all classes and code to be built. Class package diagrams are the UML equivalent of block diagrams.

Different parties think of a project according to their different needs. Programmers think in terms of language and tactical design. Architects think in terms of dependencies, risk, technology, building, testing, and OO principles. Project managers think in terms of risk, tracking, resources, need, ownership, required skills, and delivery. Although all issues are important, and good packaging recognizes its responsibility to all needs, architects tend to identify top-level packaging with an eye on the control functions of project management. For example, a project manager might draw a package diagram for a web application such as that shown in Figure 3-8.

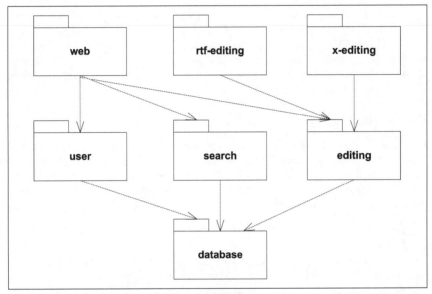

Figure 3-8. Top-level packages defining a web application

The diagram in Figure 3-8 carries very little meaning by itself. It must be accompanied by an auxiliary, textual document that describes the basis for the packaging. Such a document might, for example, contain a list as follows:

web

> Requires special skills: HTML, CSS, and Struts, a presentation technology; most dependencies.

database

> Requires database management and modeling skills; most independent/ fewest dependencies.

`user`
> To be built off-site by a remote team.

`search`
> Requires familiarity with search engine technology and techniques; self-contained subsystem.

`editing`
> Comprises the basic editing features to be delivered in the first release; different skills and different team.

`rtf-editing`
> Comprises those editing features scheduled for release 2.

`x-editing`
> Comprises editing features requested by a specific client. These features to be withdrawn or delayed depending on that client. Risk is independent of the other features.

Figure 3-8 doesn't show the complete set of packages in the system. It is merely enough for management to track and control the project. Programmers create lower-level packages as needed for correct code design. Managers, however, allocate resources and track progress on the relatively large grains of the project shown in Figure 3-8 without getting disturbed by the addition or refactoring of internal packages and contents.

Use Case Packages

Use case packages organize the functional behavior of a system during analysis. Figure 3-9 shows the major functional areas of a content management system. The packages provide understandable terms for team members outside the analyst team. Managers can discuss the project at an appropriate level of detail without getting bogged down in details.

The CMS system shown in Figure 3-9 comprises packages created for the following reasons:

- The complex editing packages separate the preliminary delivery and the advanced delivery from the client-based delivery.
- The simple interactions, view and feedback, contain basic, low-risk functions.
- The reporting has more sophisticated functions.
- The search and the user management separate complex functions.

Just as with the class packages in Figure 3-8, you manage the use case packages to manage the project. Remember that tracking use case packages tracks customer value.

Directed Dependency Graphs

Directed dependency graphs of the packages in a system reveal nonfunctional issues related to buildability, testability, and robustness; they provide a guide for several roles in software development.

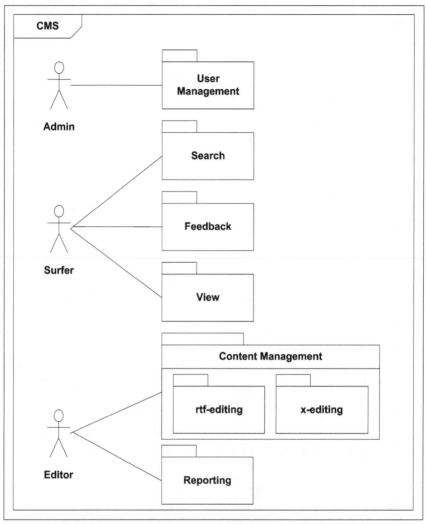

Figure 3-9. A set of functional major use case packages

When all the dependencies flow in one direction, as in Figure 3-10, without any loops or cycles, the graph is *acyclic*. Acyclic graphs show a project in good health.

Directed dependency graphs can help you avoid problems with build scripts and project testing. Looking at Figure 3-10, you can see that refactoring timer will invalidate testing and potentially break the build of visualizers, threads, controllers, and top; you should thus change the timer package with caution.

Directed dependency graphs can also help you divide project work among different staff members. For example, Figure 3-10 shows no dependencies between threads and visualizers. Thus, different groups of people can work on those two packages without destabilizing each other.

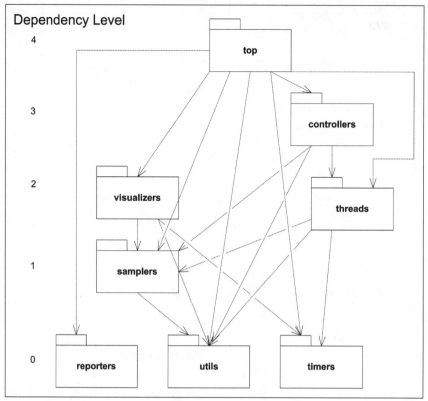

Figure 3-10. Dependency graph of modified JMeter with no cycle

Through time, projects evolve, and new dependencies creep in because of misunderstanding or expediency. Figure 3-11 shows such a case; three bidirectional dependencies ruin the desirable, acyclic nature of the graph:

- utils now depends on threads.
- threads now depends on controllers.
- samplers now depends on threads.

The problem here is that the reverse of each dependency already existed in Figure 3-10. The result is the tangle of bidirectional arrows in level 1 of Figure 3-11, which contrasts with the clear flow of arrows in Figure 3-10. The further result is pain, for the developers, testers, and likely, managers and users. Changes in threads will confound the team responsible for controllers and utils, and vice versa because fixes in one require fixes in the code or unit tests of the others. It may take several iterations until all packages stabilize.*

---

* For more theory and metrics regarding packages and their dependencies, see John Lakos' *Large-Scale C++ Software Design*. Also see Robert C. Martin's *http://c2.com/cgi/wiki?PrinciplesOfObjectOrientedDesign*.

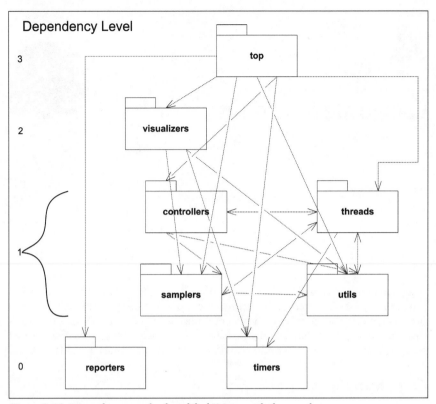

Figure 3-11. Dependency graph of modified JMeter with three cycles

4

Composite Structures

As a system becomes more complex, it is often helpful to decompose it in terms of functionality (see Chapter 7). To realize a piece of functionality, different elements of a system often work together and communicate information. UML 2.0 formalizes the concept of complex relationships between elements into the idea of composite structures. Much of the material in this chapter is new to UML 2.0.

Composite Structures

A *structure* is a set of interconnected elements that exist at runtime to collectively provide some piece of functionality. For example, you can use a structure to represent the internal makeup of a classifier such as a subsystem (what objects are related to each other, who is communicating with whom, etc.). UML calls such structures *internal structures*. UML defines several symbols to capture the relationships and communications between elements in an internal structure.

Connectors

Connectors represent communication links between instances of classes participating in an internal structure. They can be runtime instances of associations, or they can represent dynamic communication set up at runtime—for example by being values of local variables. You show a connector as a solid line between two instances. Note that while associations between classes represent a link between any instances of those classes, a connector represents a link between only the two instances specified at each end of the connector (see "Collaborations").

You can provide name and type information for a connector using the following format:

name:classname

where:

name

> Is the name of the connector. The name can be used later in collaborations to reference this connector.

classname

> Is the name of an association this connector represents.

Figure 4-1 is an example of a named connector.

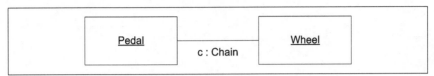

Figure 4-1. The link between a Pedal and a Wheel is a connector named "c," which is a Chain

UML specifies several rules for determining the types of the elements at each end:

- If a connector is an instance of an association, the types of the instances at either end of the connector must be the same types at either end of the association.
- If an instance at one end of a connector has required interfaces, the instance at the other end of the connector must provide one of those interfaces.
- If an instance at one end of a connector has required interfaces and a port is connected to the other end of the connector, the port must provide a required interface.

The actual means of communication isn't specified by the connector; it can represent a simple method call or a complex protocol over a socket connection. You can constrain the connection using the normal UML note notation. Simply specify the constraint in a note, and link it to the connector using a dashed line. Figure 4-2 shows a constrained connector.

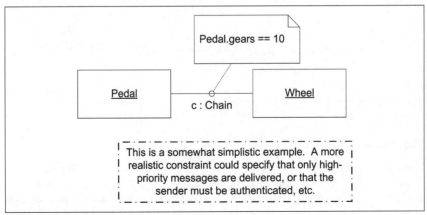

Figure 4-2. A constrained connector

You may specify the multiplicity of each *connector end* using the normal multiplicity syntax. Simply write the number of instances for a given end near the end of the connector. For example, a student/teacher relationship may require at least 5 students and no more than 20. You can show the student/teacher relationship as depicted in Figure 4-3.

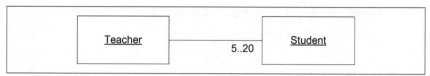

Figure 4-3. A Teacher must have at least 5 Students but no more than 20

Ports

A *port* is a way to offer functionality from a composite structure without exposing the internal details of how that functionality is realized. For example, you may have a subsystem that can perform credit card payment verification. The actual implementation of this functionality may be spread over several classes working in conjunction. The organization of these classes can be represented as an internal structure within the subsystem, and the overall functionality, or credit card verification, can be exposed using a port. Exposing the functionality through a port allows the subsystem to be used by any other classifier that conforms to the port's specifications. Starting with UML 2.0, classes have been extended to allow for ports and internal structures. By default, ports are public, however UML 2.0 allows you to have internal ports that are available only to the composite structure hosting them.

You show a port as a small square. You typically draw the name and multiplicity of the port near the square, though both may be hidden. If you draw the port on the edge of a classifier, the port is public and is available to the environment. If you draw the port inside a classifier, the port is protected and available only to the composite structure. Figure 4-4 shows an example port.

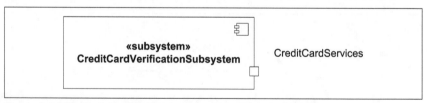

Figure 4-4. The CreditCardVerificationSubsystem with a single public port, CreditCardServices

Required and provided interfaces

Ports are associated with required and provided interfaces (see "Interfaces" in Chapter 2). Required interfaces show what the owning classifier may ask of its environment through a given port. Provided interfaces show what functionality a classifier exposes to the environment. For example, our credit card payment system may provide an interface to verify credit cards, CreditCardProcessor, while requiring access to an account verification system, AccountServices, offered by the credit card company. If you use ports in your diagrams, the required and provided interfaces capture *all* the interaction the system may have with a given classifier. Provided and required interfaces are typically shown using the ball and socket (lollipop) notation, though you may explicitly type a port (see "Port typing"). If there are multiple required or provided interfaces, simply list each interface name followed by a comma; don't show multiple lollipops. Figure 4-5 shows a port with a required interface and two provided interfaces.

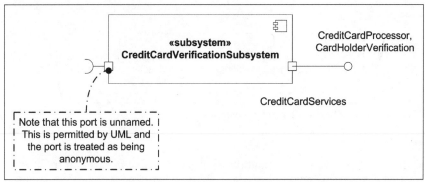

Figure 4-5. The CreditCardVerificationSubsystem providing two interfaces (CreditCardProcessor and CardHolderVerification) and requiring one (AccountServices)

Realizing port implementations

Ports are wired to an internal implementation using connectors. See "Connectors" for information on how to represent a connector. If the classifier owning the port provides the implementation of the functionality itself, the port is considered a *behavioral port*. In this case, the connector links to a state inside the classifier. This state is used to explain the behavior of the classifier when the port is used (see Chapter 8 for more information on using states to model behavior). This is typically used for simple classifiers (not complex structures) that implement functionality themselves. Figure 4-6 shows a behavioral port.

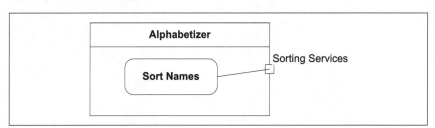

Figure 4-6. A behavioral port

On the other hand, if the functionality is realized by internal elements, you link the connector to internal classifiers that provide the implementation. This is typically used for composite structures such as components and subsystems. Figure 4-7 shows such a port.

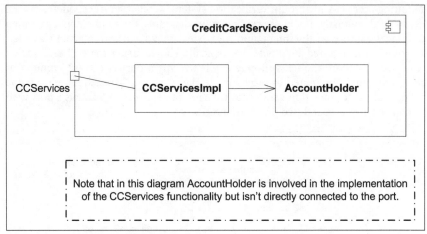

Note that in this diagram AccountHolder is involved in the implementation of the CCServices functionality but isn't directly connected to the port.

Figure 4-7. A port linked to an internal implementation

Multiple connectors

UML 2.0 allows you to have multiple connectors leading from a port to different internal elements. However, it doesn't specify what happens when communication is received at that port; this is left up to the modeler. Some possible solutions are to forward the communication to *all* connectors, forward based on priority, forward on a round-robin basis, or simply randomly choose a connector. Regardless of your decision, be sure to document it in your model, probably using a note attached to the port. Figure 4-8 shows an example of using a port with many connectors.

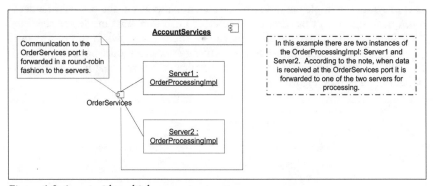

Figure 4-8. A port with multiple connectors

Port multiplicity

A classifier may specify multiplicity for a port like any other element. Simply place the desired number of port instances in brackets after the port name and type (if present). When the classifier is instantiated, the associated ports are instantiated as well. These are called *interaction points* and can be uniquely identified by the classifier. For example, if your classifier has two ports, one with provided interfaces that offer anonymous access to data and one with a provided interface that offers authenticated access to data, your classifier can distinguish which port was used by the external system. Figure 4-9 shows the credit card verification system offering two instances of the credit card verification port.

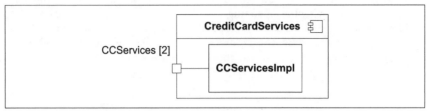

Figure 4-9. A component with two instances of the CCServices port

Port typing

In practice, when a port is instantiated, it is represented by a classifier that realizes the provided interfaces. Any communication with this interaction point simply passes the information to internal classifiers that realize the behavior. UML 2.0 allows you to specify the type of a port using classes to provide more sophisticated behavior. For example, you can specify that the port is typed using a class that filters the communications it receives or prioritizes delivery. When this port is instantiated, the corresponding class has a chance to manipulate the communication it receives before passing it to the realizing classifiers. To show that a port should be represented using a specific classifier, simply follow the name of the port with a colon and the name of the classifier to use. Note that the classifier must realize the provided interfaces. You can use this notation to show provided interfaces by using an interface as the port type, though the lollipop notation is often more flexible. Figure 4-10 shows an explicitly typed port.

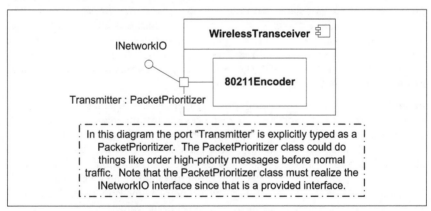

Figure 4-10. A port explicitly typed as a PacketPrioritizer

Structured Classes and Properties

As described in Chapter 3, classifiers with whole-part relationships typically use composition arrows to show their relationships. In the context of composite structures, UML 2.0 has defined the term *property* to describe the "part" piece of the whole-part relationship. For example, in a graphical operating system, an application may be made up of a main window and several buttons. The buttons are a part of the application, so that the whole-part relationship between the application and the buttons can be shown using composition. However, the main window is shared with the operating system (so the system can reposition the window or hide it); as a result, the operating-system-to-window relationship is slightly weaker and is shown using association. You can model the application, window, and button relationships as shown in Figure 4-11.

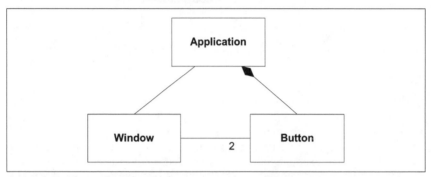

Figure 4-11. The Application, Window, Button relationship

When used in composite structure diagrams, relationships between properties are shown in the owning classifier's rectangle. This allows you to further restrict the association between parts of the composite classifier. For example, Figure 4-11 shows that Buttons can be associated with any Window. Using a composite structure diagram, you can restrict the Window to be associated only with a Button owned by the same application. When you draw the composite structure diagram, properties that are associated with the composite structure through composition are shown with solid rectangles, and properties that are shared with other structures are shown using a dashed rectangle. You may place multiplicity information for a property in its rectangle in the upper right corner, or after the name of the property in brackets. Figure 4-12 shows the composite structure diagram of application, window, and button relationships.

In addition to simply specifying how properties fit together, you can use composite structures to specify how instances are instantiated. As in Chapter 3, instances are shown by underlining the name and type of the classifier. You may specify initial values for each attribute of a classifier by specifying the name of the attribute followed by an equals sign and the value of the attribute. When used as instances, you can specify the roles each property will take on by showing a slash "/" followed by the role name after the property name and type. Figure 4-13 shows the initialization of a button with its appropriate values.

You can show that the instance of the owning classifier is related to a particular constructor of a classifier using a dependency line labeled with the keyword «create». You can use any parameters to the constructor when initializing properties simply by using the parameter name. Figure 4-14 shows the application composite diagram tied to a constructor on the Application class.

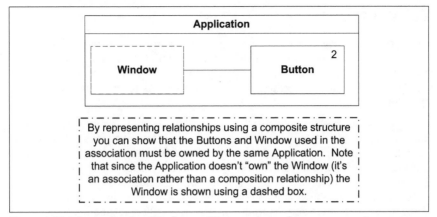

Figure 4-12. The Application, Window, and Button relationships as a composite structure

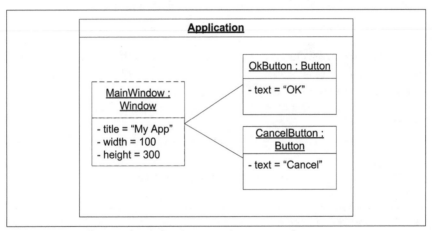

Figure 4-13. Application composite structure with property values

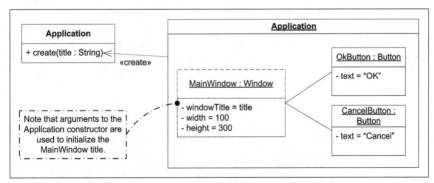

Figure 4-14. Application constructor relating to an instance of an Application

Collaborations

One of the primary purposes for composite structures is to document how a particular piece of functionality is implemented within a system. This organization of elements to realize behavior is called a *collaboration*. A collaboration is a collection of instances wired together using connectors to show the communication flow.

Because the purpose of collaborations is to describe how a particular piece of functionality works, details outside the scope of the desired functionality are typically left off a diagram. Instead, a collaboration diagram shows the required links between instances and the attributes involved in the collaboration. You may have multiple collaborations involving the same instances but showing different views of each based on the functionality expressed. One effective way of showing different views of a classifier is to use *interfaces* to collect related functionality. A single class may realize multiple interfaces, but each collaboration can focus on a single interface. See "Interfaces" in Chapter 2 for more information.

Within a collaboration, it is helpful to name the instances involved. You typically name an instance based on its role in the collaboration. For example, if you wish to model the Observer/Observable design pattern, you will likely have an instance in the role of Observer and an instance in the role of Subject.

You show a collaboration using a dashed ellipse with the name of the collaboration written inside. Figure 4-15 shows a collaboration named "Observer/Observable."

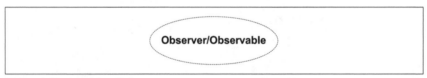

Figure 4-15. A simple collaboration

There are two ways to render the details of a collaboration. The first is to add a compartment to the collaboration ellipse and draw the instances involved in the collaboration inside. Links between instances are shown as solid lines. Each instance is named according to its role in the collaboration. Figure 4-16 shows the internal structure of the Observer/Observable collaboration.

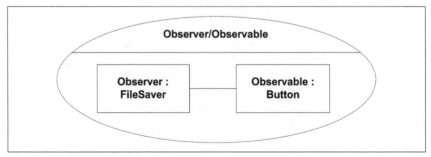

Figure 4-16. Internal details of a collaboration

Alternatively, you can show the instances that make up a collaboration outside of the collaboration ellipse and use communication links to tie them back in. In this case, you don't specify the role name inside the classifiers; instead, you write the role name along the communication link for each instance. The advantage of this notation is that you can specify the attributes and operations that are involved in the collaboration (remember, you can leave off any attribute or operation that isn't directly related to the functionality you are expressing). The disadvantage of this notation is that you don't model the direct communication paths between the various instances. Figure 4-17 shows the Observer/Observable pattern using this alternate notation.

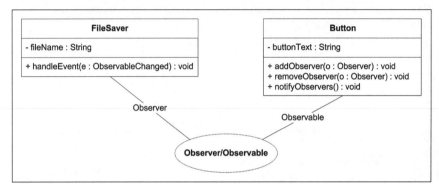

Figure 4-17. The Observer/Observable collaboration with details outside of the collaboration ellipse

The UML specification makes it clear that any classifier can be substituted for any member of the collaboration as long as they provide the appropriate attributes and operations to fulfill their role. For example, in the Observer/Observable collaboration shown in Figure 4-17, the Observable must have a means of adding, removing, and notifying observers, and the Observer must have a way to handle changes to the observable. Any other classifier may be used in this collaboration as long as it can provide the message font attribute and the appropriate operation. As mentioned earlier, interfaces lend themselves nicely to collaborations. You can define an Observable interface and programmatically capture exactly what attributes and operations are needed to fulfill a role.

UML 2.0 makes collaborations full classifiers, meaning you can attach sequence diagrams, state machines, or any other behavioral diagram to help capture the details of the implementation.

Collaboration Occurrences

UML 2.0 introduced a new concept to allow you to attach a collaboration to a specific operation or classifier to show how it is realized by other elements. When you associate a collaboration with an operation or classifier, you create a *collaboration occurrence*. You can think of collaboration occurrences as instances of collaborations. For example, you can use a collaboration occurrence to document how various classes make up a subsystem, what is responsible for persistence, what is really a façade to another subsystem, etc. The advantage of using a collaboration occurrence to document the implementation of functionality is that you can assign role names to internal elements of the classifier. There may be multiple occurrences of a particular collaboration within a classifier, each with different internal elements fulfilling the roles of the collaboration.

You show a collaboration occurrence using the same dashed ellipse used to show a collaboration, except that you list the name of the occurrence followed by a colon, and then the name of the collaboration type. For each role used in the original collaboration, you draw a dashed line from the collaboration occurrence to the element fulfilling the role. You label the dashed line with the name of the role. For example, a collaboration occurrence of our Observer/Observable collaboration is shown in Figure 4-18.

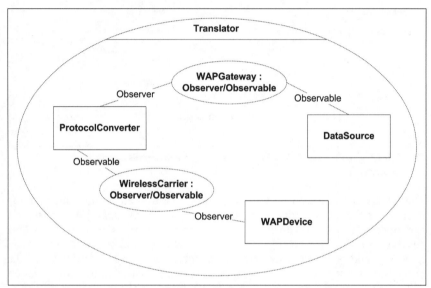

Figure 4-18. Two collaboration occurrences of the Observer/Observable collaboration

5

Component Diagrams

When modeling large software systems it is common to break the software into manageable subsystems. UML provides the *component* classifier for exactly this purpose. A component is a replaceable, executable piece of a larger system whose implementation details are hidden. The functionality provided by a component is specified by a set of *provided interfaces* that the component realizes (see "Black-Box View"). In addition to providing interfaces, a component may require interfaces in order to function. These are called *required interfaces*.

The functionality of a component's provided interfaces is implemented with one or more internal classifiers. These are typically classes but can be other components (see "White-Box View"). Components should be designed to be reused, with dependencies on external interfaces, strong encapsulation, and high cohesion.

Components

In UML 2.0, you represent a component with the classifier rectangle stereotyped as «component». Like other classifiers, if the details of the component aren't shown, you place the name of the component in the center of the rectangle. Optionally, you may show the component icon (a rectangle with two smaller rectangles on the left side) in the upper-right corner. Figure 5-1 shows a simple component.

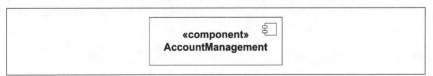

Figure 5-1. A simple component

The representation for a component has changed from previous versions of UML. UML 1.4 recognized a, rectangle with two smaller rectangles:

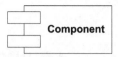

This notation is still recognized for backward compatibility but is no longer recommended.

Component Dependencies

Components may need other components to implement their functionality. You can show component dependencies using the dependency relation (a dashed line with an open arrow) between the two components. Figure 5-2 shows the AccountManagement component dependent on two other components.

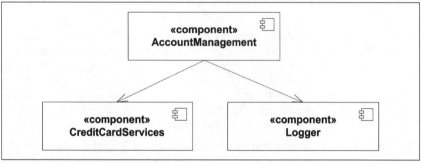

Figure 5-2. Component dependency

Representing component dependencies in this fashion is a relatively high-level view of a system. To further refine the diagram you may want to show inter-component relationships as dependencies on the interfaces provided by other dependent components (see "Black-Box View"; also see "Interfaces" in Chapter 2).

Component Views

UML uses two views of components, a black-box view and a white-box view. The *black-box view* shows a component from an outside perspective; the *white-box view* shows how a component realizes the functionality specified by its provided interfaces.

Black-Box View

The black-box view of a component shows the interfaces the component provides, the interfaces it requires, and any other detail necessary to explain the guaranteed behavior of the component. It *does not* specify anything about the internal implementation of the component. This distinction is central to the concept of replaceable components.

Assembly connectors

When modeling a black-box view of a component, you represent the provided and required interfaces using *assembly connectors*. Assembly connectors are illustrated using ball-and-socket icons. To show a required interface, use the socket icon and write the name of the interface near the connector symbol. Figure 5-3 shows a component with two required interfaces.

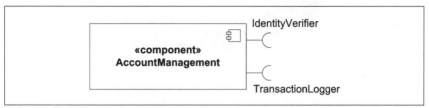

Figure 5-3. Component with two required interfaces

Show a provided interface with the ball half of an assembly connector, again with the name of the interface near the symbol. Figure 5-4 shows a component with a provided interface.

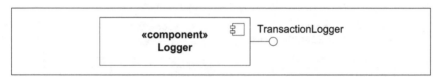

Figure 5-4. Component with a provided interface

To wire components together, simply connect the matching provided and required interfaces. Component dependencies using assembly connectors provide more details about the actual relationships between components than simple dependency relations. Figure 5-5 shows the same three components from the "Component Dependencies" section, but using assembly connectors.

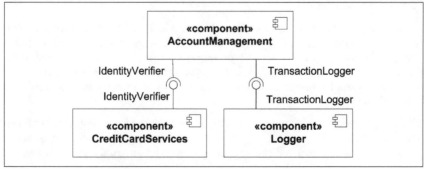

Figure 5-5. Component relationships using assembly connectors

Interface dependencies

While assembly connectors provide more detail than simple component dependencies, they don't provide detailed information about the interface that is being realized. UML provides a third black-box representation of components using realization and dependency relationships to interfaces. If a component provides an interface, use a realization arrow from the component to the interface. If the component requires an interface, use a dependency arrow from the component to the required interface. Figure 5-6 shows the same three components as Figure 5-2, but with explicit interface dependencies.

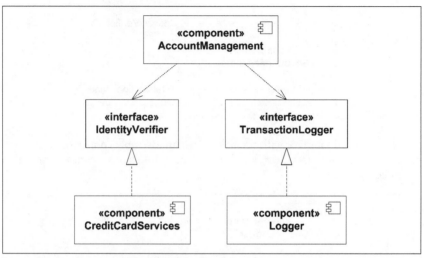

Figure 5-6. Components with explicit interface dependencies

An advantage to the interface dependency style of modeling is that you can attach other modeling elements, such as a state machine or use case, to an interface. This is particularly useful when a component implements a protocol because you can link the provided interface to a protocol state machine to further clarify the component's usage (see "Protocol State Machines" in Chapter 8).

Component compartments

UML also provides a black-box view of components using compartments. You may add a compartment to show provided and required interfaces. Label provided interfaces with the stereotype «provided interfaces» and required interfaces with the stereotype «required interfaces». Figure 5-7 shows the AccountManagement component using compartments to identify the provided and required interfaces.

UML suggests an additional compartment, stereotyped «artifacts», that can show which artifacts actually implement a component (typically one or more JARs, DLLs, etc.). Figure 5-8 shows a component with an artifact compartment.

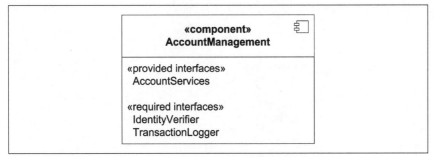

Figure 5-7. Interface dependencies in compartment form

Figure 5-8. A component with an artifacts compartment

White-Box View

In order to provide details about the implementation of a component, UML defines a white-box view. The white-box view shows exactly how a component realizes the interfaces it provides. This is typically done using classes and is illustrated with a class diagram; however a component may delegate some or all of its behavior to other components.

Realization compartment

The simplest white-box view of a component is to add a compartment to the component and list the classifiers that realize it. The compartment should be labeled with the «realizations» stereotype. While this provides more detail than a black-box view, it is of limited use to component developers. Figure 5-9 shows a component with a realizations compartment.

Classifier dependencies

To show the internals of a component, you may show each classifier that realizes a component with a dependency on the component itself. Note that the relationship between the classifiers and the component is a dependency relationship (dashed line, open arrow), not a realization relationship. This notation is useful

Figure 5-9. Component with a realizations compartment

for identifying which classifiers make up a component, but the focus of the diagram is still on the component as a whole. Figure 5-10 shows a white-box view of a component and its constituent classifiers.

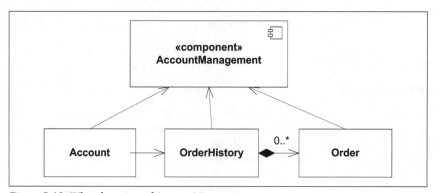

Figure 5-10. White-box view of AccountManagement

To shift the focus to the structure of the classifiers making up the component, you may show the classifiers inside the component's rectangle. This tends to have the effect of emphasizing the relationships of the classifiers making up the component, and it encourages component encapsulation. Figure 5-11 shows the detailed realization of a component.

If the internals of a component are sufficiently complex, it is common to use a separate class diagram to model the details. You can link the new class diagram back to its component using a note.

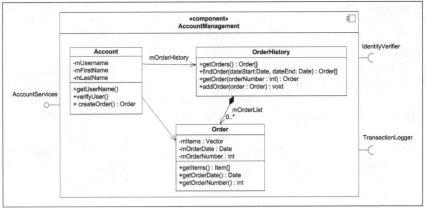

Figure 5-11. Detailed realization of AccountManagement

Ports and connectors

UML 2.0 introduces the concept of *ports* to allow you to explicitly identify functionality that is exposed to the outside world. A port groups together related provided and required interfaces and uses *connectors* to map them to a classifier that realizes the functionality. If a port has both provided and required interfaces, it is called a *bidirectional port*. A port is shown as a small rectangle on one of the sides of a classifier. An assembly connector (ball and socket) indicates provided and required interfaces.

In order to show the realization of functionality, a connector maps the port to an internal classifier. A connector is shown as a solid line with a filled arrow from the port to the classifier. A connector indicates that any messages arriving at the port (typically in the form of method calls) are forwarded to the specified classifier. You can also use connectors from a classifier to a port to show messages being passed through a provided interface. Figure 5-12 shows a white-box view of a component with three ports.

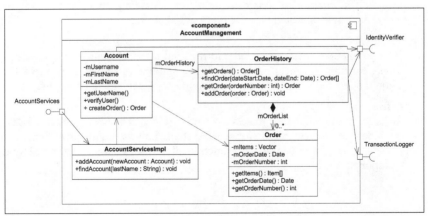

Figure 5-12. Component realization with ports and connectors

Component Stereotypes

UML defines several stereotypes that apply specifically to components:

Entity
> A component that represents a business concept. An entity component typically passes information in and out of interfaces and is often persisted as a whole. Entities don't typically have any functionality, or service capabilities, associated with them; they are usually just for data storage and retrieval.

Process
> A component that can fulfill functional requests (as opposed to an entity component). A process component is transaction-based and typically has some type of state associated with it (as opposed to stateless service components).

Realization
> A component that doesn't have its own specification. Rather it is a realization of a *specification* component, as shown in Figure 5-13.

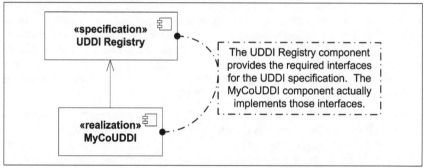

Figure 5-13. A specification component associated with a realization component

Service
> A stateless component that can fulfill functional requests. Service components are rarely persisted because they contain no state.

Specification
> A component that has provided and required interfaces but no implementation (realizing classifiers). A *specification* component, shown in Figure 5-13, should be paired with a *realization* component or implement component.

Subsystem
> A larger component that makes up part of a bigger software system. UML provides no real definition for a subsystem; however, *subsystem* generally means a self-contained set of functionality that is larger than a simple component.

6

Deployment Diagrams

Deployment diagrams model the mapping of software pieces of a system to the hardware that is going to execute it. Software elements (components, classes, etc.) are typically manifested using *artifacts* and are mapped to the hardware or software environment that will host them, called *nodes*. Because many nodes may be associated with the deployment of a system, communication between nodes can be modeled using *communication paths*.

Artifacts

Artifacts represent physical pieces of information related to the software development process. For example, you can use an artifact to represent a DLL needed by your system, a user's manual, or an executable produced when your software is compiled.

Typically artifacts are used to represent the compiled version of a component (see Chapter 5); however, UML 2.0 allows artifacts to represent any packageable element, which includes just about everything in UML. You show an artifact using the classifier rectangle with a dog-eared paper in the upper right. Figure 6-1 shows a basic artifact.

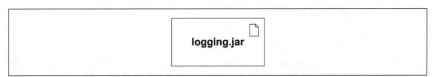

Figure 6-1. A simple artifact

UML allows artifacts to have properties and operations that manipulate the artifact. These are most commonly used when an artifact represents a set of configurable options. For example, *deployment specifications*, which represent configuration settings for deployed artifacts, frequently use attributes to represent the allowed settings (see "Deployment Specifications"). Figure 6-2 shows an artifact with attributes.

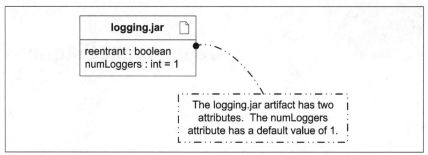

Figure 6-2. An artifact with attributes

Artifact Instances

Like nearly all other UML classifiers, artifacts are really *types*. This means that technically a physical DLL on a node is an *instance* of an artifact. For example, you can have an artifact named logging.jar that represents your logging framework implementation. However, you may have several web applications installed on a server, each with their own copy of logging.jar. Each physical copy is an instance of the original artifact.

You show an instance of an artifact by underlining the name of the artifact. Figure 6-3 shows an instance of the logging.jar artifact.

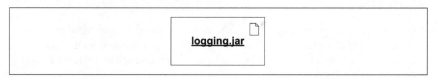

Figure 6-3. An instance of the logging.jar artifact

Typically you can determine whether an artifact is intended to be a type or an instance based on context, so UML allows the normal (nonunderlined) representation of an artifact to be interpreted as an instance of that artifact if the context is clear. Practically speaking, this translates into most models using artifacts as instances, but not underlining the title.

Manifestations

An artifact is a *manifestation* of another UML element. For example, logging.jar may be a manifestation of the LoggingSubsystem component. You capture the manifestation relationship with a dashed line from the artifact to the element it represents, and label the line with the keyword «manifest». Figure 6-4 shows the LoggingSubsystem manifestation.

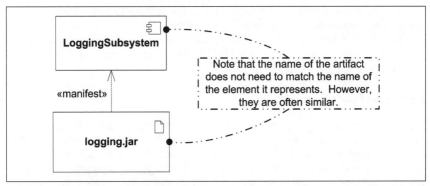

Figure 6-4. Showing the manifestation of a component as an artifact

In UML 1.x, manifestations were known as *implementations*. In UML 2.0 it was decided that *implement* had been overused, so it has been deprecated in favor of the keyword manifest.

Nodes

A node is a physical entity that can execute artifacts. Nodes can vary in size from a simple embedded device to a server farm. Nodes are a critical piece of any deployment diagram because they show where a particular piece of code executes and how the various pieces of the system (at the execution level) communicate.

You show a node as a 3D box with the name of the node written inside. However, possibly more than any other classifier in UML, modelers typically use specific icon representations of nodes to help convey the type of hardware represented. Figure 6-5 shows a simple node as a cube, as well as example icon representations.

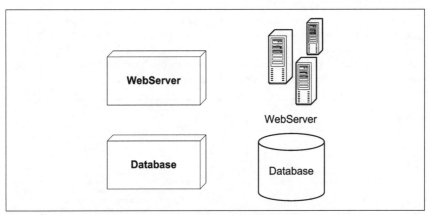

Figure 6-5. Several nodes using the cube representation, and some example icon representations

Previous versions of UML did not define any specializations of a node. UML 2.0 specializes a node into two different aspects of hosting code: the *required software* and the *required hardware*. Therefore, it is less common to see a generic node in UML 2.0 diagrams than it was in UML 1.x. See "Execution Environments" and "Devices" for more information.

Execution Environments

An *execution environment* is a specialized node that represents a software configuration hosting specific types of artifacts. An execution environment is expected to provide specific services to hosted artifacts by means of mutually agreed upon interfaces. For example, a Java 2 Enterprise Edition (J2EE) application expects to run in a software environment called an Application Server. The J2EE specification enumerates several services that should be provided by an Application Server, such as database connectivity, lifecycle contracts, and resource location. You can express that a node is an Application Server (and therefore provides the required services) by defining a stereotype for the node. For example, a typical stereotype for an Application Server is J2EE Container. Figure 6-6 shows an Application Server execution environment.

Figure 6-6. A J2EE execution environment

You can specify how services provided by the execution environment are configured using configuration files or deployment specifications (see "Deployment Specifications").

An execution environment is technically a node by itself but is typically shown as part of another, hardware-based node. For example, a J2EE Container may itself be hosted on a machine named AppServer1. You can show the hosting relationship by embedding the execution environment in the hardware node, or by using a composition arrow. Figure 6-7 shows both representations.

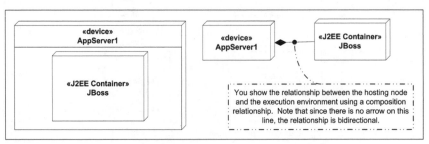

Figure 6-7. Two representations of an execution environment in a node

Execution environment stereotypes

The UML specification intends for people to create UML 2.0 Profiles that define unique execution environments and their required deployment specifications. These unique environments are each given their own stereotype and are applied to nodes when appropriate. For example, the UML specification suggests stereotypes such as «OS», «database system», and «J2EE Container».

Explicit services

Usually, any services offered by the execution environment are implicit in the stereotype used. However, you may explicitly show the services if that increases the readability of your model. The specification doesn't state how to represent explicit services but suggests listing them in a compartment within the execution environment. Figure 6-8 shows an example execution environment with an explicit list of the services offered.

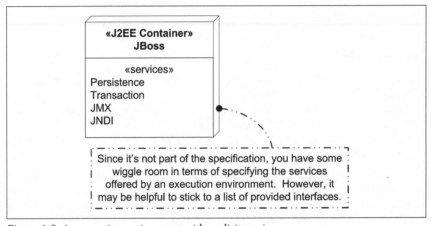

Figure 6-8. An execution environment with explicit services

Devices

A *device* is a specialization of a node that represents a physical machine capable of performing calculations. There are no implied size restrictions on a device; a device can be an embedded controller or the hardware the controller is installed in.

You show a device as a node with the stereotype «device». Figure 6-9 shows a node stereotyped as a device.

Figure 6-9. A node stereotyped as a device

One of the more powerful features of devices is that they can be nested. For example, you can model a server with internal devices representing RAID controllers, video cards, etc. A real-world use of nested devices can be pixel and vertex shading code running on a video card (represented as a device) while the rest of the application runs on the machine's CPU. Figure 6-10 shows an example of what this diagram might look like.

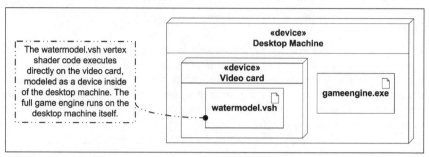

Figure 6-10. A device (the video card) nested inside another device (the desktop machine)

Communication Paths

Communication paths represent generic communication between nodes. For example, a router may pass HTTP requests to a web server that uses a proprietary socket connection to a database. Assuming the database is hosted on its own machine, you can model the deployment of the system as nodes linked via communication paths. The concept of links between nodes existed prior to UML 2.0, however now the specification formally names them.

You show a communication path as a solid line drawn from one node to another. You typically don't show any directionality on the line because the communication is assumed to be bidirectional. Figure 6-11 shows an example web server configuration with several nodes communicating over communication paths.

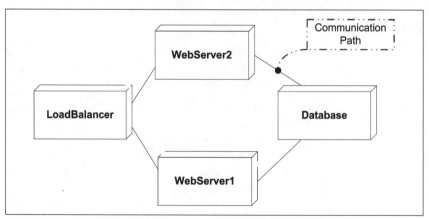

Figure 6-11. Several nodes linked with communication paths

UML doesn't specify a way of modeling the actual messages passed between nodes. However, protocol state machines (see Chapter 8) often provide a good way to represent information flow if a particular protocol is spoken between nodes. If a link represents messages between components that aren't captured in a protocol state machine, it may make sense to link to one or more component diagrams (see Chapter 5) using a note. Figure 6-12 shows an example communication path linked to a component diagram.

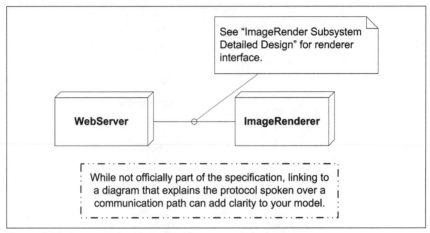

Figure 6-12. A communication path with a note attached

Deployment

The most important aspect of deployment diagrams is conveying the relationship between artifacts and the node(s) they execute on. When you associate an artifact with a *deployment target* (anything that can host an artifact, such as a device or execution environment), you *deploy* that artifact. For example, you may have an artifact named ccvalidator.jar that represents the credit card validation subsystem of an application. When you say ccvalidator.jar executes on the node Appserver1, you have deployed the artifact.

Deployment Representation

UML provides several ways to show deployment. You may show artifact deployment by simply drawing an artifact in the hosting node's cube. Figure 6-13 shows an artifact named ccvalidator.jar deployed to the device Appserver1.

UML also allows you to show deployment using a dashed line with an open arrow (dependency) pointing from the artifact to the deployment target. You should stereotype this line with the keyword «deploy». Figure 6-14 shows the same deployment relationship as Figure 6-13, but uses the dependency notation.

Finally, you may show deployment by simply listing deployed artifacts in a compartment in the deployment target's classifier. This notation is particularly useful if you have a lot of artifacts deployed to a single node. Figure 6-15 shows an execution environment with several deployed artifacts.

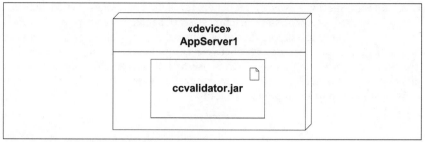

Figure 6-13. An artifact deployed to a device

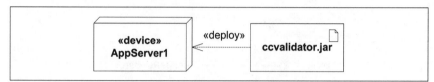

Figure 6-14. Artifact deployment using a dependency relationship

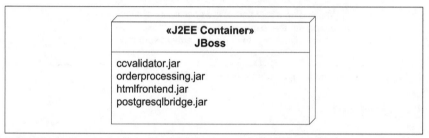

Figure 6-15. An execution environment with a list of the deployed artifacts

UML 2.0 introduced the term *deployed artifact* for artifacts that have been associated with nodes. There is no new notation; UML 2.0 just added a formal recognition of the concept.

Deployment Specifications

A *deployment specification* is a collection of properties that specify how an artifact is to be deployed on a deployment target. For example, you can specify that an artifact requires database transactions or connection information to communicate with a server. You model the specific deployment information as a deployment specification artifact.

You show a deployment specification using the classifier rectangle stereotyped as «deployment spec», with required deployment information as attributes. Figure 6-16 shows an example deployment specification captured in a file named *web.xml*.

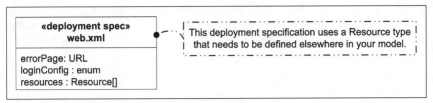

Figure 6-16. A sample deployment specification

The specific information in a deployment specification depends on the type of artifact being deployed. You may need a separate model to capture the type of information used by the specification. For example, Figure 6-16 uses a type named Resource that should be defined on another diagram.

It's common to bundle an artifact and its deployment specification into a larger artifact. You show the relationship between an artifact and its deployment specification using a dashed line with an open arrow (dependency) pointing from the specification to the artifact. Figure 6-17 shows bundling the weatherserver.jar application with its deployment descriptor in a web archive called weatherserver.war.

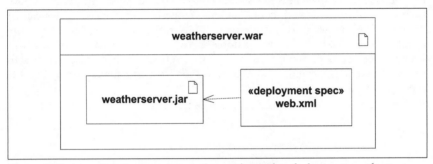

Figure 6-17. An artifact that contains another artifact and its deployment specification

Variations on Deployment Diagrams

Most of the time deployment diagrams are used for their intended purpose: to show how an application is physically deployed. Some modelers prefer to display the bare minimum, just showing how many machines they will need and how they are supposed to talk. Modelers often take liberties with the official notation and will specify minimum requirements for their machines, as in Figure 6-18.

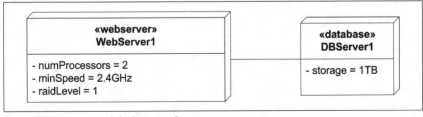

Figure 6-18. A minimal deployment diagram

Obviously Figure 6-18 doesn't provide any information on actual software deployment. Instead of focusing on the node's configuration, you can focus on the software deployment configuration and specify details for executing your software, as shown in Figure 6-19.

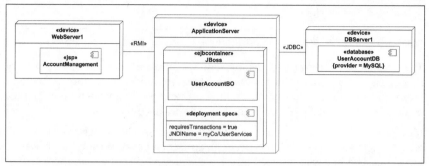

Figure 6-19. Detailed application deployment diagram

For the sake of completeness, we should mention that deployment diagrams have been used to show network configurations. Properties and tagged values can be used to show network configuration options rather than machine hardware details. Figure 6-20 shows an example network modeled as a deployment diagram. Be warned, though: deployment diagrams were not designed with network modeling in mind, so a professional network administrator may find the syntax lacking.

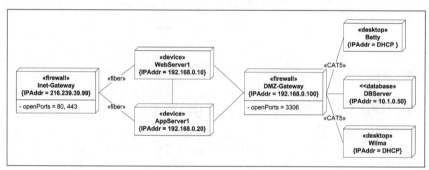

Figure 6-20. A sample network topology using a deployment diagram

7

Use Case Diagrams

Use cases are a way to capture system functionality and requirements in UML. Use case diagrams consist of named pieces of functionality (*use cases*), the persons or things invoking the functionality (*actors*), and possibly the elements responsible for implementing the use cases (*subjects*).

Use Cases

Use cases represent distinct pieces of functionality for a system, a component, or even a class. Each use case must have a name that is typically a few words describing the required functionality, such as View Error Log. UML provides two ways to draw a use case. The first is an oval with the name of the use case in the center. Figure 7-1 shows a basic use case.

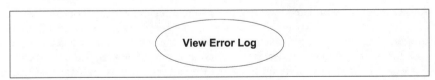

Figure 7-1. A simple use case

You can divide a use case's oval into compartments to provide more detail about the use case, such as extension points (see "Use Case Extension"), included use cases (see "Use Case Inclusion"), or the modeling of specific constraints. Figure 7-2 shows a use case oval with a compartment listing extension points.

However, the oval representation of use cases doesn't hold up well with detailed compartments. UML recommends you use the classifier notation if you want to provide details about a use case. Show the use case as a rectangle, with the use case oval in the top-right corner. Now, place the name of the use case in the top, in bold. You can then divide the classifier into compartments as needed. Typical

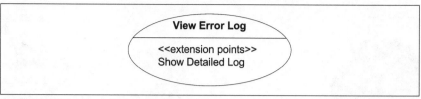

Figure 7-2. Use case with a compartment showing extension points

compartment names are extension points and included use cases. Figure 7-3 shows the same use case as in Figure 7-2, but in classifier notation.

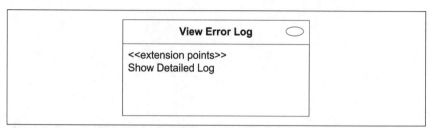

Figure 7-3. Use case in classifier notation

UML makes a clear distinction that the term *use case* strictly applies to the UML element and its name. Full documentation of a use case is considered an *instantiation* of the use case. This is a subtle distinction, but it allows you to document a use case whatever way best captures the use case's functionality. You can document a use case in a text document, state machine, interaction diagram, activity diagram, or anything else that conveys the details of the functionality in a meaningful way to your reader.

Actors

A use case must be initiated by someone or something outside the scope of the use case. This interested party is called an *actor*. An actor doesn't need to be a human user; any external system or element outside of the use case may trigger the use case (or be the recipient of use case results) and should be modeled as an actor. For example, it is very common to model the system clock as an actor that triggers a use case at a given time or interval.

An actor can have several different representations in UML. The first is a stick figure with the name of the actor written near the icon (usually right below it). Figure 7-4 shows an actor icon.

Alternatively, an actor can be shown using the classifier notation. You represent the actor with a rectangle, with the keyword actor at the top and the name of the actor in bold immediately below that. Because actors don't typically have compartments, this representation isn't used very often. Figure 7-5 shows an actor in classifier notation.

If it is helpful, you may use custom icons to clearly distinguish different types of actors. For example, you can show an external database system using a database

Figure 7-4. An actor using the stick figure representation

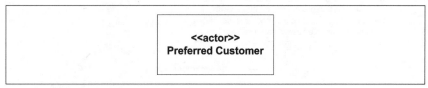

Figure 7-5. An actor using classifier notation

icon while showing the system administrator as a stick figure. Figure 7-6 shows exactly this set of actors.

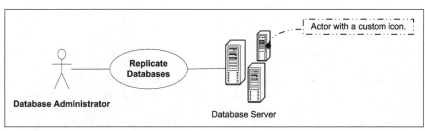

Figure 7-6. Actor with a custom icon

Actor/Use Case Associations

You typically associate an actor with one or more use cases. A relationship between an actor and a use case indicates the actor initiates the use case, the use case provides the actor with results, or both. You show an association between an actor and a use case as a solid line. Conventionally you read use case diagrams from left to right, with actors initiating use cases on the left and actors that receive use case results on the right. However, depending on the model or level of complexity, it may make sense to group actors differently. Figure 7-7 shows an actor communicating with a use case.

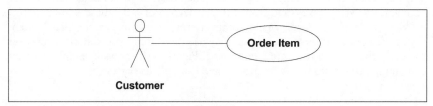

Figure 7-7. An actor associated to the Order Item use case

Though not part of the official UML specification, it is common to see directional arrows on association lines to indicate who initiates communication with whom. Note that the arrows don't necessarily restrict the direction of information flow; they simply point from the initiator to the receiver of the communication. What happens after a use case begins execution is specified elsewhere (see "Use Cases"). Figure 7-8 shows two actors and a use case with directional associations.

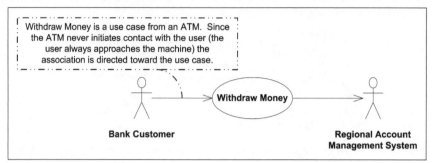

Figure 7-8. An example of directed associations between actors and a use case

System Boundaries

By definition, use cases capture the functionality of a particular subject. Anything not realized by the subject is considered outside the system boundaries and should be modeled as an actor. This technique is very useful in determining the scope and assignment of responsibilities when designing a system, subsystem, or component. For example, if while you are modeling an ATM system, your design discussions digress into discussions of the details of the back-end banking system, a use case model with clearly defined system boundaries would identify the banking system as an actor and therefore outside the scope of the problem.

You represent system boundaries in a generic sense using a simple rectangle, with the name of the system at the top. Figure 7-9 shows the system boundaries for the ATM machine mentioned in the previous paragraph.

Using Actors to Identify Functionality

Actors don't need to have a one-to-one mapping to physical entities; in fact, they don't need to be physical entities at all. UML allows for actors to represent roles of potential users of a system. For example, the system administrator may be the only *physical* user of a system, but that administrator may wear many hats. It may be helpful to view the system from the perspective of a database administrator, backup administrator, deployment administrator, and so on. By specifically identifying the various roles of actors that may use the system, you can often discover use cases that would have gone unnoticed. Figure 7-10 shows a sample diagram containing three types of administrators and example use cases.

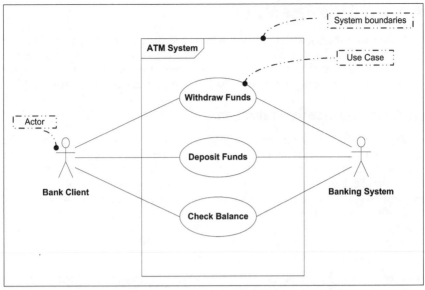

Figure 7-9. A use case diagram showing the system boundaries of an ATM System

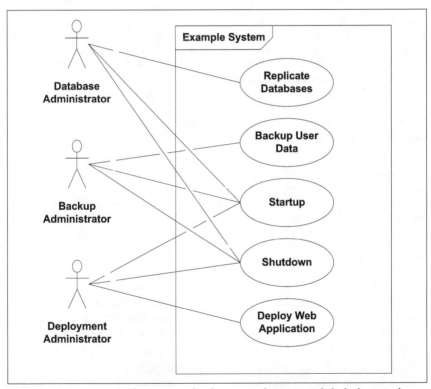

Figure 7-10. An example of using specialized versions of an actor to help find required functionality

Advanced Use Case Modeling

As it does for other classifiers, UML provides mechanisms for reusing and adding on to use cases and actors. You can expand an actor's capabilities or replace entire use cases using *generalization*. You can factor out common elements of use cases using *included* use cases, or add on to base use cases using use case *extension*.

Actor and Use Case Generalization

Though not officially mentioned in the specification, actors and use cases can be generalized like many other classifiers. Actor generalization is typically used to pull out common requirements from several different actors to simplify modeling. For example, Figure 7-10 shows several administrators and the use cases they need to invoke. You may have a Database Administrator, a Backup Administrator, and a Deployment Administrator, all with slightly different needs. However, the majority of the needs of the individual actors may overlap. You can factor out a generic System Administrator actor to capture the common functionality, and then specialize to identify the unique needs of each actor.

You represent actor generalization like any other classifier; draw a solid line, with a closed arrow pointing from the specialized actor to the base actor. Figure 7-11 shows the same information as Figure 7-10 but in a much easier-to-read diagram.

Use cases may be generalized as well. Typically use case generalization is used to express some high-level functional need of a system without going into specifics. Specializations of a general use case introduce specific functionality. For example, a generic use case can be Verify Passenger Identity, and specializations of that use case can be Check Passenger Fingerprint and Verify Passenger's RFID Tag. It is important to notice that even with use case generalization, you should still discuss functionality, not implementation. You should not have specializations of a use case for different ways to implement the *same functionality*, only to represent *different functionality*.

You represent use case generalization just like you do actor generalization: using a solid line, with a closed arrow pointing from the specialized use case to the base use case. If the general use case represents abstract functionality (meaning it's a functional concept but doesn't actually explain how a user would do something), you show the name of the use case in italics. Figure 7-12 shows the verification use cases and their relationships.

Use Case Inclusion

You can factor out common functionality from several use cases by creating a shared, included use case. Unlike in use case extension (discussed next), the use case that includes another use case is typically not complete on its own. The included functionality isn't considered optional; it is factored out simply to allow for reuse in other use cases.

You show use case inclusion using a dashed line, with an open arrow (dependency) pointing from the base use case to the included use case. Label the line with the keyword include. Figure 7-13 shows an example of use case inclusion.

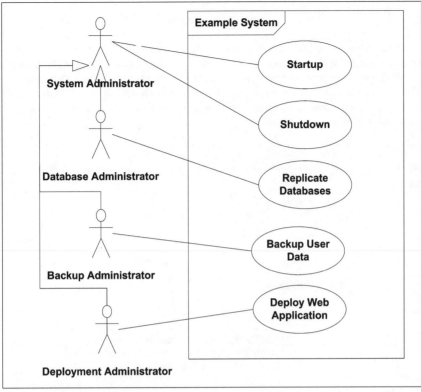

Figure 7-11. Actor generalization, in which the System Administrator is the generic base actor and the lower three are specializations

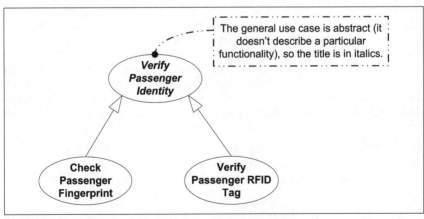

Figure 7-12. Use case generalization

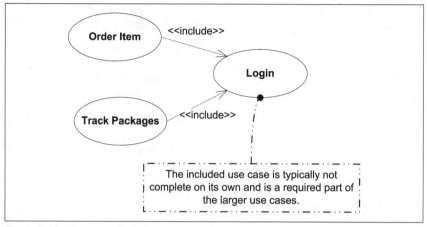

Figure 7-13. Use case inclusion

Use Case Extension

UML provides the ability to plug in additional functionality to a base use case if specified conditions are met. For example, if you are modeling a banking application, you can have a use case named Open Account that specifies how the user can create a new account with the bank. You can offer a joint account that allowed a user to add other people to his account. The joint account functionality can be captured with a different, use case named Add Joint Member. In this case the specified condition for the extension is more than one member on the bank application.

UML clearly specifies that a base use case should be a complete use case on its own. The extension use cases are typically smaller in scope and represent additional functionality, so they may not be useful outside the context of the base use case.

Any use case you want to extend must have clearly defined *extension points*. An extension point is a specification of some point in the use case where an extension use case can plug in and add functionality. UML doesn't have a particular syntax for extension points; they are typically freeform text, or step numbers if the use case functionality is represented as a numbered list.

You list extension points in a use case oval, or in a separate compartment when using the classifier notation. Figure 7-14 shows a use case with extension points.

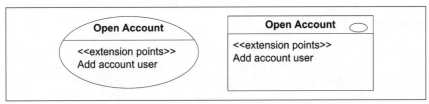

Figure 7-14. Oval and classifier notation for a use case with extension points

You represent a use case extension by showing a dashed line, with an open arrow (dependency) pointing from the extension use case to the base use case. Label the line with the keyword extend. Figure 7-15 shows an example of use case extension.

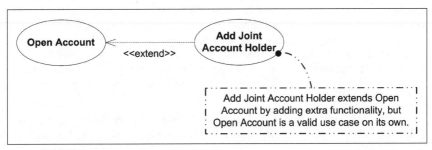

Figure 7-15. Use case extension

To provide more detail you can specify where the new functionality plugs into the base use case by specifying an extension point and a note attached to the dependency line. Optionally you can specify under what condition the extension executes, such as applicants > 1. Figure 7-16 shows use case extension with a note specifying the extension point and the condition to execute the extra functionality.

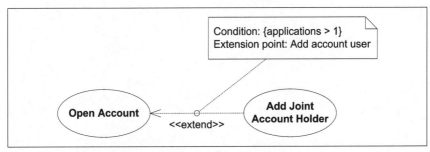

Figure 7-16. Use case extension showing conditions in a note

When the system encounters an extension point in a use case, any conditions associated with extension use cases are evaluated. If a condition is met, the corresponding extension functionality is executed. Once all appropriate extension use cases have been executed, the base use case continues with the next step in the original flow.

Use Case Scope

As mentioned previously, a use case is a distinct piece of functionality, meaning it is of sufficient granularity that the user has accomplished his desired goal. Proper scoping of use cases is an art, but UML sets several requirements to make the job a little easier:

* A use case must be initiated by an actor.
* When a use case is considered complete, there are no further inputs or outputs; the desired functionality has been performed, or an error has occurred.
* After a use case has completed, the system is in a state where the use case can be started again, or the system is in an error state.

One popular rule of thumb is to ask yourself if the user can "go to lunch" after completing the use case, meaning that a reasonably sized goal has been achieved by the initiator. For example, Add item to shopping cart is probably not the larger goal a user intends; Purchase item is likely a better scope. Purchase item can consist of adding an item to a shopping cart but typically has more functionality such as logging on, entering billing and shipping information, and confirming the order.

Above all, use cases are intended to convey desired functionality, so the exact scope of a use case may vary depending on the intended audience and purpose for modeling.

Statechart Diagrams

State machine diagrams capture the behavior of a software system. State machines can be used to model the behavior of a class, subsystem, or entire application. They also provide an excellent way of modeling communications that occur with external entities via a protocol or event-based system.

UML has two types of state machines:

Behavioral state machines
> Show the behavior of model elements such as objects. A behavioral state machine represents a specific implementation of an element.

Protocol state machines
> Show the behavior of a protocol. Protocol state machines show how participants may trigger changes in a protocol's state and the corresponding changes in the system (i.e., the new state of the protocol). Protocol state machines aren't typically tied to a particular implementation, and they show the required protocol behavior.

Behavioral and protocol state machines share common elements; however, protocol state machines are not tied to an implementation and have restrictions on their transitions. Because protocol state machines are a specialization of behavioral state machines, this chapter first discusses behavioral state machines and other topics common to all state machine diagrams; then details of protocol state machines are explained.

Behavioral State Machines

State machines represent the behavior of a piece of a system using graph notation. A state machine is shown using the basic rectangle notation, with the name of the state machine shown in the top compartment. The outside rectangle is often omitted on state machine diagrams that show only a single state machine. The

metaclass is simply *state machine*. Figure 8-1 shows a simple state machine
modeling a soda machine.

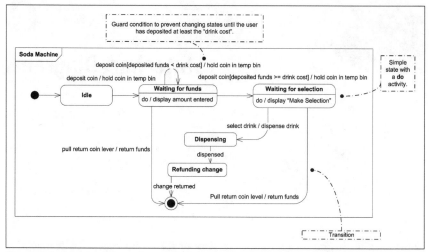

Figure 8-1. A basic state machine

A state machine is often associated with a classifier in the larger UML model—for
example, a class or subsystem. However, UML doesn't define a specific notation
to show this relationship. One possible notation is to use a note labeled with the
name of the state machine and linked to the classifier. Figure 8-2 shows an
example that uses a note to link a state machine to a classifier.

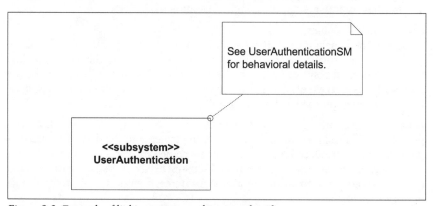

Figure 8-2. Example of linking a state machine to a classifier

You can model the behavior of the classifier using *states*, *pseudostates*, *activities*,
and *transitions*. If a state machine is used to model the behavior of an operation
(see "Operations" in Chapter 2), the state machine must have parameters that
match the operation's parameters. These can be used in any transition or state as
needed.

Transitions between states occur when *events* are dispatched (see "Dispatch"). As the state machine executes, activities are run based upon the transition, entry into a state, and so on (see "Activities").

Each state machine has a set of *connection points* that define the external interface to the state machine. These connection points must be either *Entry* or *Exit* pseudostates.

States

States model a specific moment in the behavior of a classifier. This moment in time is defined by some condition being true in the classifier.

States model a situation in the behavior of a classifier when an *invariant condition* holds true. Put more simply, a state is a "condition of being" for the state machine and, by association, the classifier that's being modeled. For example, a coffee machine could be "Grinding Beans," "Brewing," "Warming Coffee," "Dispensing," etc. A state can represent a static situation, such as "Waiting for Username" or a dynamic situation where the state is actively processing data, such as "Encrypting Message."

A state is shown as a rectangle with rounded corners. The name of the state is written inside the rectangle. Figure 8-3 shows a simple state.

Figure 8-3. A simple state

A state name may be placed outside of the rectangle in a tab notation when showing composite or submachine states (see "Composite States" and "Submachine States"). You should either use the tab notation or place the name inside the state; don't do both. Figure 8-4 shows a state using a tab for the state name.

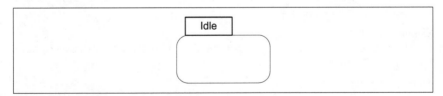

Figure 8-4. A state with its name in a tab

Within the rectangle a state can be divided into compartments as needed. UML defines the following compartments:

Name
   Shows the name of the state. This should not be used if the name is placed in a tab.

Internal activities

> Shows a list of internal activities that are performed while in the state. See "Activities" for the syntax.

Internal transitions

> Shows a list of internal transitions (see "Transitions") and the events that trigger them. Write an internal transition as:
>
> event (*attributeList*) [*guard condition*]/ *transition*
>
> The attribute list, which is optional, maps the event's parameters to the given attributes of the classifier. The guard condition is also optional, but, if present, must be enclosed by square brackets.
>
> The same event may be listed multiple times as long as each entry has a unique guard condition for the transition.

Figure 8-5 shows a state with compartments.

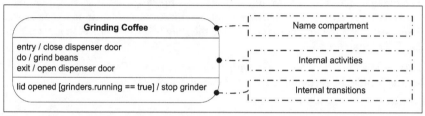

Figure 8-5. A state with compartments

A state can be either *active* or *inactive*. A state is considered active as soon as it is entered because of some transition. Similarly, a state is considered inactive immediately after leaving the state.

UML defines three types of states:

Simple states

> Simplest of all states, they have no substates. All the example states used so far in this section are simple states.

Composite states

> Have one or more regions for substates. A composite state with two or more regions is called *orthogonal*.

Submachine states

> Semantically equivalent to composite states, submachine states have substates that are contained within a *substate machine*. Unlike composite states, submachine states are intended to group states, so you can reuse them. Composite states are typically specific to the current state machine.

Composite and submachine states are explained in more detail in the following subsections.

Composite States

A composite state is a state with one or more regions. A *region* is simply a container for substates. A composite state with two or more regions is called *orthogonal*.

A composite state may have an additional compartment called the decomposition compartment. A *decomposition compartment* is a detailed view of the composite state where you can show a composite state's regions, substates, and transitions. Figure 8-6 shows a composite state with a single region.

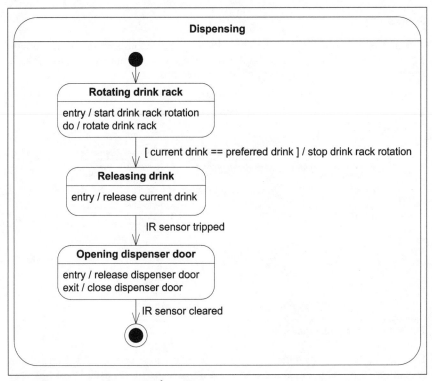

Figure 8-6. A composite state with one region

You may hide the decomposition compartment to increase the clarity of a diagram. If you hide the compartment, you can use the composite icon to indicate that the state's decomposition isn't shown on this diagram. Figure 8-7 shows a composite state with the decomposition compartment hidden.

Figure 8-7. Composite state with composite icon

You may place states within a region of a composite state to represent internal substates. A substate that isn't contained in another state is called a *direct substate*, and a substate contained within other substates (resulting in recursive, composite states) is called an *indirect substate*.

A composite state is considered active when the state machine is in any of the composite's substates. When a composite state is active, the tree of active states, starting with the composite state itself and working down to the current substate, is called the *state configuration*. For example, a state configuration for Figure 8-6 could be Dispensing->Releasing drink.

Regions

A region is shown using a dashed line dividing the decomposition compartment. You may name each region by writing its name within the region's area. Figure 8-8 shows a composite state with two regions.

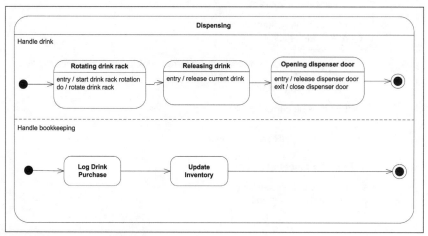

Figure 8-8. A composite state with two regions

Each region has its own *initial pseudostate* (see "Pseudostates") and a *final* state. A transition to a composite state is a transition to the initial pseudostate in each region. Each region within a composite state executes in parallel, and it is perfectly acceptable for one region to finish before another. A transition to the final state of a region indicates completing the activity for that region. Once all regions have completed, the composite state triggers a completion event and a completion transition (if one exists) triggers.

Submachine States

Submachine states are semantically equivalent to composite states in that they are made up of internal substates and transitions. UML defines a submachine state as a way to encapsulate states and transitions so that they can be reused. A submachine state simply means that another state machine, a submachine state machine, is contained by the state. For example, the process of establishing a TCP/IP connection can be encapsulated into its own state machine, and that state machine can then be embedded as the first submachine state of a state machine modeling a web page request.

A submachine state is shown in the same rounded rectangle as any other state, except you show the name of the state, followed by a colon (:), followed by the name of the referenced submachine. Figure 8-9 shows a submachine state.

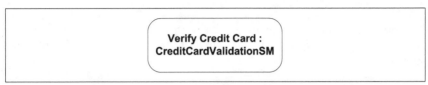

Figure 8-9. A submachine state referencing the credit card validation state machine

Typically when showing a submachine state you show the entry and exit points of the referenced submachine. You show these points as pseudostates on the border of the submachine state (see "Pseudostates"). Figure 8-10 shows a submachine state with an explicit exit point.

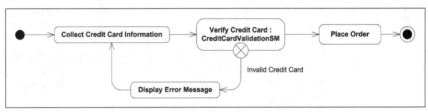

Figure 8-10. Credit card validation submachine state with explicit exit point

If the submachine state is entered through the default initial pseudostate or exited because of the completion of the submachine, you don't need to show explicit entry/exit points. The state machine shown in Figure 8-10 uses the default initial pseudostate and two different exit points. A submachine state machine may be used multiple times within a containing state machine, and different references to the submachine may show different entry/exit points based on what is relevant to the current submachine state.

For clarity you may use the same *composite icon* to show that the referenced submachine is defined elsewhere in the model. Figure 8-11 shows a submachine state with the composite icon.

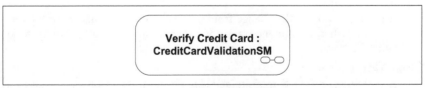

Figure 8-11. A submachine state showing the composite icon

Transitions

A transition shows the relationship, or path, between two states or pseudostates. It represents the actual change in the configuration of a state machine as it heads from one state to the next. Each transition can have a guard condition that indicates if the transition can even be considered (*enabled*), a trigger that causes the transition to execute if it is enabled, and any effect the transition may have when it occurs.

Transitions are shown as a line between two states, with an arrowhead pointing to the destination state. You specify the details of the transition using the following syntax:

> *trigger* [*guard*] / *effect*

where:

trigger
> Indicates what condition may cause this transition to occur. The trigger is typically the name of an event, though it may be more complex.

guard
> Is a constraint that is evaluated when an event is fired by the state machine to determine if the transition should be enabled. Guards should not have any side effects and must evaluate to a boolean. Guards will always be evaluated before a transition is fired. The order in which multiple guards are evaluated isn't defined. A guard can involve tests of states in the current state machine—for example, not in Dialing or in WaitingForCall. The state names can be fully qualified if necessary.

effect
> Specifies an activity that is executed when a transition happens. This activity can be written using operations, attributes, and links of the owning classifier as well as any parameters of the triggering event. An *effect* activity may explicitly generate events such as sending signals or invoking operations.

Figure 8-12 shows several transitions between states.

Transition types

UML defines several specific types of transitions. These are described in the following list. There are no special symbols associated with transition types. They are defined only for clarity and common vocabulary.

Compound transition
> A representation of the change from one complete state machine configuration to another. Compound transitions are a set of transitions, choices, forks, and joins leading to a set of target states.

High-level transition
> A transition from a composite state. If the destination of the transition is outside the composite state, all the substates are exited, and their exit activities are run, followed by the exit activity of the composite state. If the transition ends with a target inside the composite state, the exit activity of the composite state isn't run.

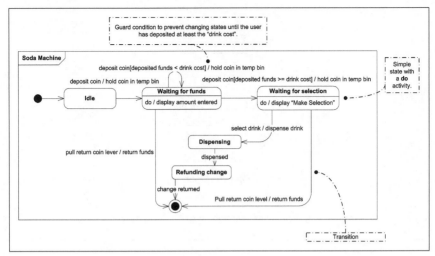

Figure 8-12. A state machine with several transitions

Internal transition

A transition between states within the same composite state. The containing state isn't exited or reentered during the transition. A transition directly from one region of a composite state to another region in the same composite state isn't allowed.

Completion transition

A transition from a state that has no explicit trigger. When a state finishes its do activities, a completion event is generated. This event is placed in the event pool and dispatched before any other event (see "Event Processing"). If the completion transition's guard conditions (if there are any) are met, the transition is triggered. You can have multiple completion transitions, however they must have mutually exclusive guard conditions. A completion transition from an orthogonal composite state will be taken when all the regions have reached their final state and have completed their do activities.

Signal symbols

Transitions may be shown in more detail using explicit icons to show signal sending, signal receipt, and effect activities. These icons are not necessary and are simply used to provide a more transition-oriented view of a state machine.

You can show a transition that receives a signal by showing an unlabeled transition from the source state to a rectangle with a triangular notch on one side. The signal's signature is shown inside the rectangle. Complete the diagram by showing an unlabeled transition pointing from the rectangle to the target state. Figure 8-13 shows a detailed view of a transition receiving a signal.

You can show a transition that sends a signal as part of the transition effect by drawing an unlabeled transition pointing from the source state to a rectangle with a triangular point on one side. The signature of the signal (including parameters) is shown inside the rectangle. Another unlabeled transition links the rectangle to the target state. Figure 8-14 shows a detailed view of a transition sending a signal.

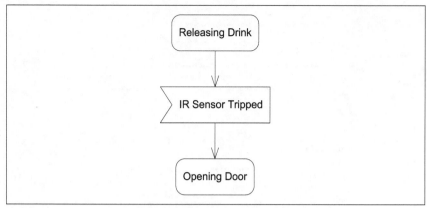

Figure 8-13. A transition-oriented view showing a signal being received

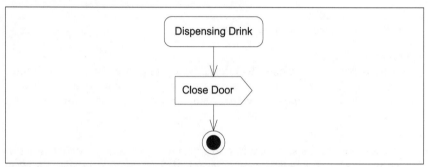

Figure 8-14. Transition-oriented view of a signal being dispatched

You can show effects that occur as a result of a transition using a simple rectangle. The description of the activity is written inside the rectangle. As with signal icons, you link everything together with an unlabeled transition from the source state to the rectangle, and then from the rectangle to the target state. Figure 8-15 shows details of the effects of a transition.

Transitions and composite states

A transition from an external state to the border of a composite state is called *default entry*. The entry activity of the composite state is executed, and then the default transition to a substate occurs.

A transition from an external state to a specific substate of a composite state is called *explicit entry*. The entry activity for the composite state is executed before the substate becomes active.

Whenever a state machine transitions to an *orthogonal composite state* (a composite state with two or more regions), each region is entered either explicitly or by default. If the composite state is entered through an explicit entry, any other region is entered using its default transition.

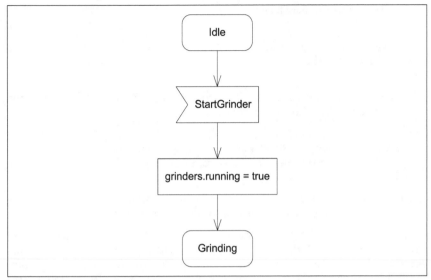

Figure 8-15. Transition-oriented view with an activity

When leaving a composite state the exit activities for the active substates are executed from the inside out. In other words, the deepest of the active substate's exit activities executes first, and then its containing substate, and so on.

When exiting an orthogonal composite state, the active substate in each region is exited first; the exit activity for the composite state is then executed.

Activities

An activity represents some functionality that is executed by a system. A state can have activities that are triggered by transitions to and from the state or by events raised while in the state. A state's activities execute only if the state is active.

Each activity has a label showing when the activity executes, and an optional activity expression. An activity is written as:

```
label / activity expression
```

You can write an activity expression using pseudocode:

```
list.append(keystroke) ; print("*")
```

or natural language:

```
record keystroke and show password character
```

You may omit the slash when you don't show the activity expression. Activity expressions can use attributes and operations available to the classifier owning the state machine.

UML reserves three activity labels:

Entry

> Triggers when a state is entered. The entry activity executes before anything else happens in the state.

Exit

> Triggers when leaving a state. The exit activity executes as the last thing in the state before a transition occurs.

Do

> Executes as long as a state is active. The do activity executes after the entry activity and can run until it completes, or as long as the state machine is in this state.

Each state may have additional activities associated with it, and specific labels for each. See Figure 8-5 for an example of a state with several activities.

If the do activity completes, it causes a *completion event*, which can trigger a transition (see "Dispatch"). If there is a *completion transition* (a transition with no other event condition), the exit activity executes, and the transition occurs. If some other event causes the state to transition before the do activity completes, the activity is aborted, the exit activity executes, and the transition occurs.

State Machine Extension

Like many other concepts in UML, state machines may be specialized as needed. A specialized state machine is an extension of a general state machine. You can specialize a state machine by adding regions, states, pseudostates, or transitions. In addition to adding features to state machines you can redefine states, regions, and transitions.

When drawing a specialized state machine, draw the inherited states with dashed or gray-toned lines. You may also place the keyword extended in curly braces after the name of the state machine. Figure 8-16 shows a specialized soda dispensing state machine. The Dispensing Drink state is extended to introduce a new substate, Out of selection. The states Releasing drink and Refunding change retain their other transitions, and a new transition, Time expired, is added to transition to the new substate if the IR sensor isn't triggered (see Figure 8-6 for the original composite state).

Protocol State Machines

Protocol state machines capture the behavior of a protocol, such as HTTP or a challenge-response speakeasy door. They aren't tied to a particular implementation of a protocol; rather, they specify the state changes and events associated with a protocol-based communication.

Unlike in behavioral state machines, states in protocol state machines represent stable situations where the classifier isn't processing any operation and the user knows its configuration.

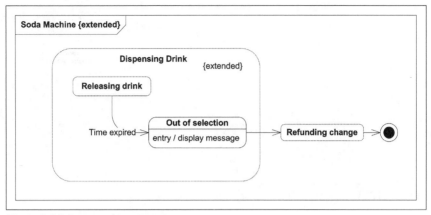

Figure 8-16. State machine extension

Protocol state machines differ from behavioral state machines in the following ways:

- entry, exit, and do activities can't be used.
- States can have invariants. Place invariants in square brackets under the state name.
- The keyword protocol is placed in curly braces after the state machine name to indicate the state machine is a protocol state machine.
- Transitions in protocol state machines have a precondition (in place of the guard in normal transitions), the trigger, and a post condition. The notation for a protocol transition is as follows:

    [*precondition*] *event* / [*postcondition*]

- Each transition is associated with zero or one operation on the owning classifier. The transition guarantees that the precondition will be true before the operation is invoked, and that the post condition will be true before entering the target state.
- The effect activity is never specified for a protocol transition.

Figure 8-17 shows a simplified version of the Simple Mail Transport Protocol (SMTP) protocol. Because protocol state machines don't not allow activities, there is little detail about what the SMTP server actually does when receiving a command from the client. By design, the protocol state machine tells you only what state the protocol implementation will be in, not what it does to get there or how it keeps itself occupied. See "Variations on Statechart Diagrams" for an example of modeling a protocol in more detail.

Pseudostates

Pseudostates are special types of states that represent specific behavior during transitions between regular states. Combined with basic transitions, pseudostates can represent complex state changes within a state machine.

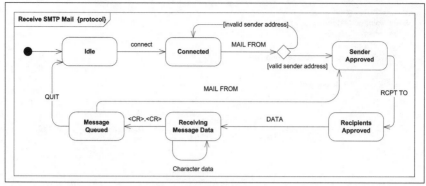

Figure 8-17. A simplified SMTP protocol state machine

Table 8-1 shows the types of pseudostates and their symbols. Refer to Figure 8-1 for an example showing how these symbols are used.

Table 8-1. Types of pseudostates

Pseudostate name	Symbol	Description
Initial pseudostate	●	The starting point of a state machine. The transition from the initial pseudostate to the first full state may be labeled with the event that instantiates the object the state machine is modeling.
Choice	◇	Allows the execution of a state machine to choose between several different states based on guard conditions on the transitions (see Figure 8-17).
Deep history	(H*)	Used inside a state region, a transition to this pseudostate from outside the region indicates the state machine should resume the last substate it was in within the given region, no matter how "deep" the substate is within the region.
Entry point	○	Represents a possible target for a transition into a composite state. An entry point can then transition to an internal substate that may differ from the default transition. You must label entry points by writing their name next to the symbol.
Exit point	⊗	Represents a possible source for a transition from a composite state. Like entry points, exit points are labeled with their names.
Fork and join	▮	Represents a split in the execution of the state machine into orthogonal regions. The join reunites the regions into a single transition. The state machine won't transition from the join until all regions have transitioned to the join pseudostate.
Junction	●	Brings several possible transitions together into one pseudostate. One or more transitions may then leave the junction to other states.

Table 8-1. Types of pseudostates (continued)

Pseudostate name	Symbol	Description
Shallow history	(H)	Used inside a state region, a transition to this pseudostate from outside the region indicates the state machine should resume the last substate it was in within the given region, however the substate must be at the same level as the history pseudostate. You may specify a default "previous state" by showing a single transition from the shallow history pseudostate to an internal substate. This is used only if the region has never been entered.
Terminate node	X	Causes the state machine to terminate.

Event Processing

Information within a state machine is conveyed via events. Events can be triggered by things outside of the state machine or as part of an activity executing within a state. An event can have parameters and attributes you can use when processing the event.

Dispatch

As events are triggered, they are added to an event pool. Once added to the event pool, events are sent out for processing by the state machine or are *dispatched*. The order of event dispatch and processing isn't specified by UML. This allows state machines to impose their own prioritization schemes on events if desired.

When dispatching events, a new event is dispatched and processed only after the previous event has been fully processed. This doesn't mean that all do activities (see "Activities") are complete, just that the state machine is in a well-defined condition, with entry and exit activities completed. This is called *run-to-completion* by the UML specification.

After an event is dispatched, if no transitions are enabled and the event isn't deferred (see "Deferred Events"), the event is discarded, and the next event can be processed.

If an event does trigger one or more transitions, such as in the case of orthogonal states (see "Composite States"), the order in which the transitions are fired isn't specified by UML. Once all transitions have been fired, the event is considered complete.

If a synchronous activity is triggered by a transition, the event processing isn't complete until the invoked object has finished its run-to-completion step.

When dispatching events, UML allows for transitions to conflict. However, only one out of a set of conflicting transitions is allowed to execute. If an event triggers two different transitions from the same state, the state machine must select only one transition to execute. The following rules determine which transition executes:

- A transition starting from a substate has higher priority than a transition from any of its containing states, and therefore is executed.
- Transitions from an orthogonal state are considered to have the same priority (assuming they are at the same level), so the first transition encountered is executed.

Deferred Events

You can list events that should be *deferred* from dispatching while in a given state. You show a deferred event by listing the event, followed by a forward slash and the keyword defer within the state. Figure 8-18 shows a state that defers the cancel event. If the cancel event does fire, it is held in the event pool until the state machine leaves this state.

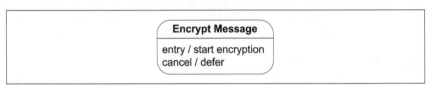

Figure 8-18. State with deferred cancel event

If an event is triggered that doesn't cause a transition, and it is on the deferred list, it will be held in an event pool while nondeferred events are dispatched. The event will be held in the pool until the state machine enters a state in which the event is no longer deferred, or in which the event would cause a transition. The event is then dispatched.

To clarify, events that cause a transition can't be deferred. If the state machine enters a state that doesn't defer an event, and the event doesn't cause a transition, the event is lost.

Variations on Statechart Diagrams

In addition to modeling behavior and protocols, statecharts have been used to capture real-time system behavior. As they do with many applications of UML diagrams, real-time system modelers frequently use tagged values and constraints to customize the syntax for their organization; however, almost all real-time diagrams include some notation to indicate time. A common notation is to use the keyword after to indicate a maximum allowable time for a transition to occur. Figure 8-19 shows a satellite uplink acquisition statechart that requires a ground station to respond to satellite commands within a fixed amount of time to prevent the acquisition sequence from failing and starting over.

Since real-time systems are frequently involved in well-defined protocols, the line between real-time state machines and protocol state machines can blur. There is no real notational difference; it is a matter of what the modeler is trying to convey. Real-time state machines often model the internal states of a system, something

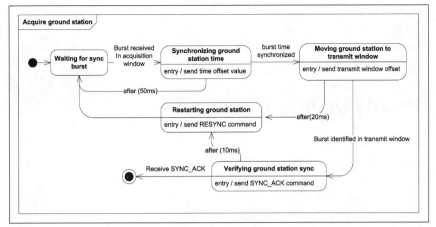

Figure 8-19. A sample real-time statechart diagram

deliberately avoided by protocol state machines. If the modeler doesn't capture the internal states of a system, or if the implementation is simple enough that there are no additional internal states, the state machine can wind up being a model of the protocol. Figure 8-19 is closer to a protocol state machine than a detailed implementation model; each state in the figure can be represented by one or more smaller, internal states in a real implementation. However, according to the strict definition of protocol state machines, *entry* activities can't be used, so Figure 8-19 isn't tagged with the {protocol} tag.

9

Activity Diagrams

Activity modeling focuses on the execution and flow of the behavior of a system, rather than how it is assembled. Possibly more than any other UML diagram, activity diagrams apply to much more than just software modeling. They are applicable to just about any type of behavioral modeling; for example, business processes, software processes, or workflows. Activity diagrams capture *activities* that are made up of smaller *actions*.

When used for software modeling, activities typically represent a behavior invoked as a result of a method call. When used for business modeling, activities may be triggered by external events, such as an order being placed, or internal events, such as a timer to trigger the payroll process on Friday afternoons. Activity diagrams have undergone significant changes with UML 2.0; they have been promoted to first-class elements and no longer borrow elements from state diagrams.

Activities and Actions

An activity is a behavior that is factored into one or more actions. An action represents a single step within an activity where data manipulation or processing occurs in a modeled system. "Single step" means you don't break down the action into smaller pieces in the diagram; it doesn't necessarily mean the action is simple or atomic. For example, actions can be:

- Mathematical functions
- Calls to other behaviors (modeled as activities)
- Processors of data (attributes of the owning object, local variables, etc.)

Translating these into real examples, you can use actions to represent:

- Calculating sales tax
- Sending order information to a shipping partner
- Generating a list of items that need to be reordered because of low inventory

When you use an activity diagram to model the behavior of a classifier, the classifier is said to be the *context* of the activity. The activity can access the attributes and operations of the classifier, any objects linked to it, and any parameters if the activity is associated with a behavior. When used to model business processes, this information is typically called *process-relevant data*. Activities are intended to be reused within an application, and actions are typically specific and are used only within a particular activity.

You show an activity as a rectangle with rounded corners. Specify the name of the activity in the upper left. You can show parameters involved in the activity below the name. Alternatively, you can use *parameter nodes*, described later in this section. Figure 9-1 shows a simple activity.

Figure 9-1. A simple activity with no details

You can show the details for an activity inside of the rectangle, or, to simplify a diagram, leave off the surrounding rectangle altogether. You show actions using the same symbol as an activity: a rectangle with rounded corners; place the name of the action in the rectangle. Figure 9-2 shows some actions inside of an activity.

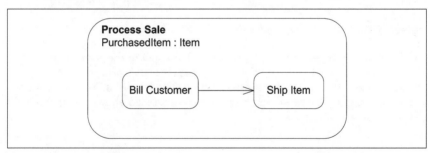

Figure 9-2. Activity with simple details

To make activity diagrams more expressive, you can write pseudocode or application-dependent language inside an action. Figure 9-3 shows an example of an action with a domain-specific block of code.

Each activity typically starts with an initial node and ends with an activity final node. When an activity reaches an activity final node, the activity is terminated. You show an initial node as a black dot and an activity final node as a solid circle

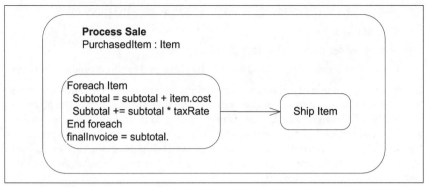

Figure 9-3. An action with pseudocode

with a ring around it. See "Control Nodes" for more information on initial and final nodes. Figure 9-4 shows an activity with initial and final nodes.

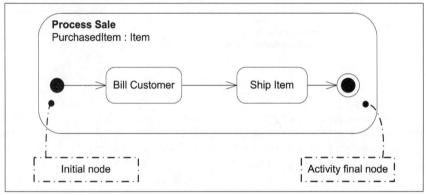

Figure 9-4. An activity diagram with initial and final nodes

Activities may have pre- and postconditions that apply to the entire activity. You show a precondition by placing the keyword «precondition» at the top center of the activity and then place the constraint immediately after it. You show a post-condition using the keyword «postcondition». Figure 9-5 shows an activity with pre- and postconditions.

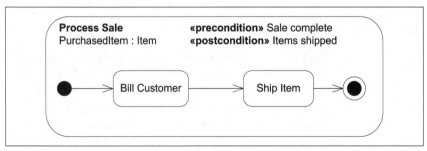

Figure 9-5. Activity diagram with pre- and postconditions

An action may have local pre- and postconditions that should hold true before the action is invoked and after it has completed, respectively. However, the UML specification doesn't dictate how pre- and postconditions map to implementation; violations of the conditions are considered implementation-dependent and don't necessarily mean the action can't execute.

You show pre- and postconditions using notes attached to the action. You label the note with the keyword «localPrecondition» or «localPostcondition». Figure 9-6 illustrates this.

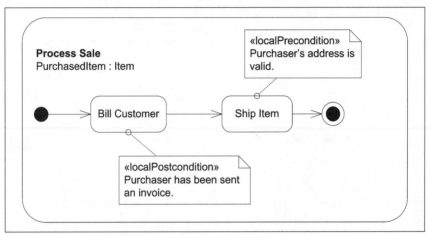

Figure 9-6. An activity diagram with local pre- and postconditions for actions

Activity Edges

In order to show flow through an activity, you link actions together using *activity edges*. Edges specify how control and data flow from one action to the next. Actions that aren't ordered by edges may execute concurrently; the UML specification leaves it up to the specific implementation of an activity diagram to say whether actions actually execute in parallel or are handled sequentially.

You show an activity edge as a line with an arrow pointing to the next action. You can name edges by placing the name near the arrow, though most edges are unnamed. Figure 9-6 (as well as the earlier figures) shows an activity diagram with several activity edges.

Control flows

UML offers a specialized activity edge for control-only elements, called a *control flow*. A control flow explicitly models control passing from one action to the next. In practice, however, few people make the distinction between a generic activity edge and a control flow because the same notation is used for both.

Object flows

UML offers a data-only activity edge, called *object flows*. Object flows add support for multicasting data, token selection, and transformation of tokens. The notation for object flows is the same as that for a generic activity edge.

You can use an object flow to select certain tokens to flow from one activity to the next by providing a *selection behavior*. You indicate a selection behavior by attaching a note to the object flow with the keyword «selection» and the behavior specified. Figure 9-7 shows selecting the top candidates from potential new hires. See "Object Nodes" for details on modeling objects.

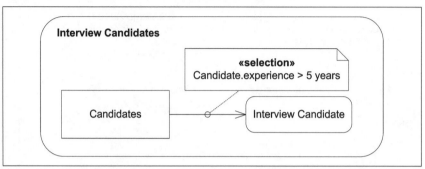

Figure 9-7. Activity diagram where objects are selected based on a selection behavior

You can assign behaviors to object flows that transform data passed along an edge; however, the behavior can't have any side effects on the original data. You show *transformation behaviors* using a note attached to the object flow. Label the note with the keyword «transformation», and write the behavior under the label. Figure 9-8 shows an example of a transformation behavior that extracts student identification from course registrations to verify that the student's account is fully paid.

Object flows allow you to specify sending data to multiple instances of a receiver using *multicasting*. For example, if you are modeling a bidding process, you can show a Request for Proposal (RFP) being sent to multiple vendors and their responses being received by your activity. You show sending data to multiple receivers by labeling an object flow with the keyword «multicast», and you show data being received from multiple senders by labeling an object flow with the keyword «multireceive». Figure 9-9 shows an activity diagram modeling an RFP process.

There are times when an action may accept more than one type of valid input to begin execution. For example, a human resources action named Adjust Salary may require an Employee object and either a New Hire Document or Yearly Performance Review Document, but not both. You can show groups and alternatives for input pins (see "Pins" under "Object Nodes") by using *parameter sets*. A parameter set groups one or more pins and indicates that they are all that are needed for starting or finishing an action. An action can use input pins only from one parameter set for any given execution, and likewise output on only one output parameter set. You show a parameter set by drawing a rectangle around

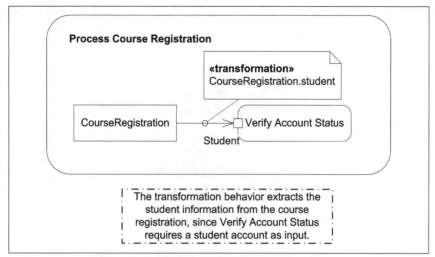

Figure 9-8. Activity diagram with a transformation behavior to traverse an object and extract the needed information

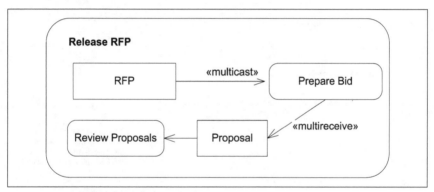

Figure 9-9. Multicast object flows

the pins included in the set. Figure 9-10 shows the Adjust Salary action with parameter sets.

Connectors

To simplify large activity diagrams you can split edges using *connectors*. Each connector is given a name and is purely a notational tool. You place the name of a connector in a circle and then show the first half of an edge pointing to the connector and the second half coming out of the connector. Figure 9-11 shows two equivalent activity diagrams; one with a connector and one without.

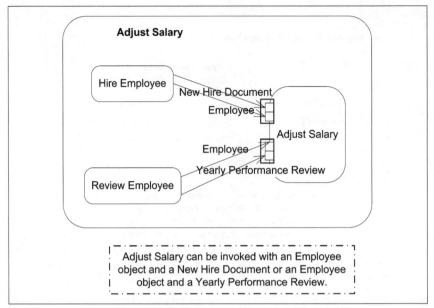

Figure 9-10. Action with parameter sets

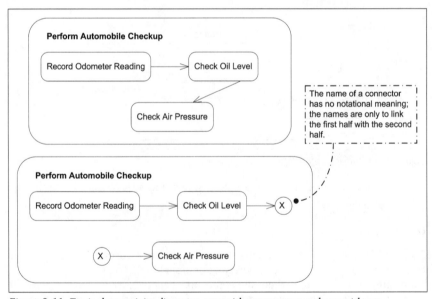

Figure 9-11. Equivalent activity diagrams, one with a connector and one without

Tokens

Conceptually, UML models information moving along an edge as a token. A token may represent real data, an object, or the focus of control. An action typically has a set of required inputs and doesn't begin executing until the inputs are met. Likewise, when an action completes, it typically generates outputs that may trigger other actions to start. The inputs and outputs of an action are represented as tokens.

Each edge may have a weight associated with it that indicates how many tokens must be available before the tokens are presented to the target action. You show a weight by placing the keyword weight in curly brackets ({}) equal to the desired number of tokens. A weight of null indicates all tokens should be made available to the target action as soon as they arrive. For example, Figure 9-12 shows that nine players are needed before you can make a baseball team.

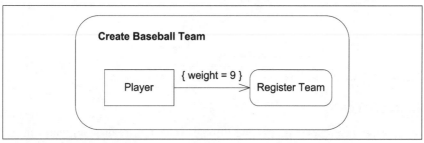

Figure 9-12. Activity diagram with edge weights

In addition to weights, each edge may have a *guard condition* that is tested against all tokens. If the guard condition fails, the token is destroyed. If the condition passes, the token is available to be consumed by the next action. If a weight is associated with the edge, the tokens aren't tested against the guard condition until enough tokens are available to satisfy the weight. Each token is tested individually, and if one fails, it is removed from the pool of available tokens. If this reduces the number of tokens available to less than the weight for the edge, all the tokens are held until enough are available. You show a guard condition by putting a boolean expression in brackets ([]) near the activity edge. Guard conditions are typically used with decision nodes to control the flow of an activity (see "Decision and merge nodes").

Activity Nodes

UML 2.0 defines several types of activity nodes to model different types of information flow. There are parameter nodes to represent data being passed to an activity, object nodes to represent complex data, and control nodes to direct the flow through an activity diagram.

Parameter Nodes

You can represent parameters to an activity or output from an executed activity as *parameter nodes*. You show a parameter node as a rectangle on the boundary of an activity, with the name or description of the parameter inside the rectangle. Input parameter nodes have edges to the first action, and output parameter nodes have edges coming from the final action to the parameter node. Figure 9-13 shows an example of wood being fed into a paper production activity, and paper being produced at the end.

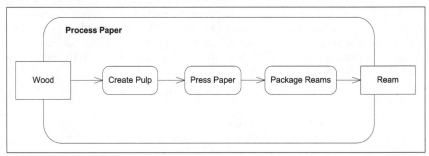

Figure 9-13. Activity diagram with incoming and outgoing parameters

Object Nodes

To represent complex data passing through your activity diagram, you can use *object nodes*. An object node represents an instance of a particular classifier in a certain state. Show an object node as a rectangle, with the name of the node written inside. The name of the node is typically the type of data the node represents. Figure 9-14 is an activity diagram showing a factory producing parts for shipping.

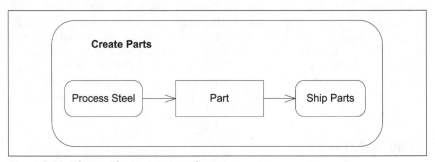

Figure 9-14. Object nodes in an activity diagram

If the type of data the node represents is a signal, draw the node as a concave pentagon. See Figure 9-37 in "Interruptible Activity Regions" for an example of a signal in an activity diagram.

Pins

UML defines a special notation for object nodes, called *pins*, to provide a short-hand notation for input to or output from an action. For example, because the action Ship Parts in Figure 9-14 requires a Part, you can define an *input pin* on Ship Parts labeled Part. You show a pin using the same rectangle as for object nodes, except the rectangle is small and attached to the side of its action. If it is an input pin, any edges leading into the action should point to the input pin; if it is an output pin, any edges leaving the action should leave from the pin. Figure 9-15 shows the Create Parts diagram rewritten using pins.

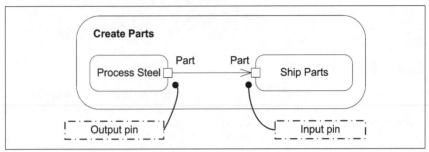

Figure 9-15. Actions with input and output pins

If the output from an action is related to an exception (error condition), you indicate that the pin is an *exception pin* by inserting a small arrow near the pin. Figure 9-16 shows the Create Parts action with error handling.

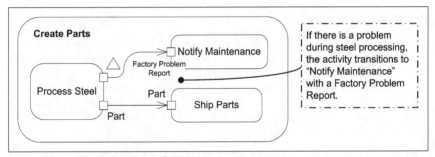

Figure 9-16. Activity diagram with an exception pin

If you don't have edges leading into or out of an action, you can show whether a pin is an input pin or an output pin by placing small arrows inside the pin rectangle. The arrow should point toward the action if you are showing an input pin and away from the action if you are showing an output pin. Figure 9-17 shows an action with input and output pins.

If an action takes a constant value as input, you can model the input data using a *value pin*. A value pin is shown as a normal input pin, except the value of the object is written near the rectangle. Figure 9-18 shows an activity diagram with a value pin.

Figure 9-17. Action with input and output pins

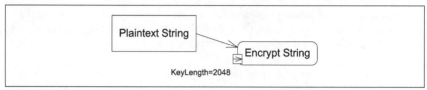

Figure 9-18. Action with a value pin

Control Nodes

In addition to actions, activities may include other nodes to represent decision making, concurrency, or synchronization. These specialized nodes are called *control nodes* and are described in detail in this section.

Initial nodes

An *initial node* is the starting point for an activity; an initial node can have no incoming edges. You can have multiple initial nodes for a single activity to indicate that the activity starts with multiple flows of execution. You show an initial node as a solid black dot, as shown in Figure 9-4.

Decision and merge nodes

A *decision node* is a control node that chooses different output flows based on boolean expressions. Each decision node has one input edge and multiple outgoing edges. When data arrives at the decision node, a single outgoing edge is selected, and the data is sent along that edge. A decision node usually selects an edge by evaluating each outgoing edge's *guard condition*. A guard condition is a boolean expression that tests some value visible to the activity, typically an attribute of the owning classifier or the data token itself.

You show a decision node as a diamond with the flows coming into or out of the sides. You show guard conditions by putting a boolean expression in brackets ([ ]) near the activity edge. Figure 9-19 is an activity diagram showing a decision made while wrapping presents.

Guard conditions aren't guaranteed to be evaluated in any particular order, and a decision node allows only one outgoing edge to be selected. You should take care to design your models so that only one guard condition ever evaluates to true for a given set of data, to prevent race conditions.

You can specify functionality that executes whenever data arrives at the decision node. Called *decision input behavior*, this functionality is allowed to evaluate the data arriving at the node and offers output for the guard conditions to evaluate. The behavior *is not* allowed to have any side effects when executing, since it can

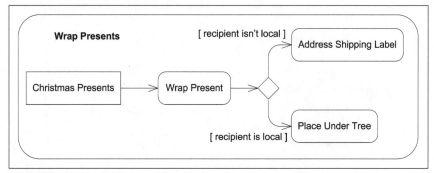

Figure 9-19. Activity diagram with a decision node

be executed multiple times for the same data input (once for each edge that needs to be tested). You show decision input behavior in a note labeled with the keyword «decisionInput». Figure 9-20 shows an activity diagram that checks to see if a newly authenticated user is the 100th user and should therefore be prompted to take a survey.

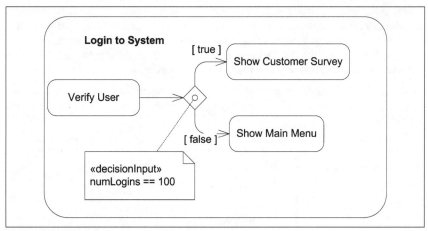

Figure 9-20. Decision node with an input behavior

A *merge node* is effectively the opposite of a decision node; it brings together alternate flows into a single output flow. It doesn't synchronize multiple concurrent flows; see "Fork and join nodes" for concurrency support. A merge node has multiple incoming edges and a single outgoing edge. A merge node simply takes any tokens offered on any of the incoming edges and makes them available on the outgoing edge.

You show a merge node using the same diamond you use in a decision node, except with multiple incoming edges and a single outgoing edge. Figure 9-21 shows how a potential new hire's information may be submitted to Human Resources for processing.

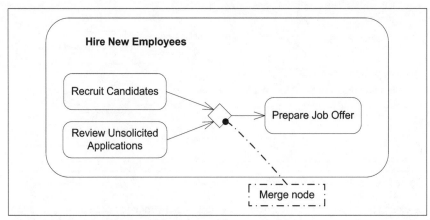

Figure 9-21. Activity diagram with a merge node

Fork and join nodes

A *fork node* splits the current flow through an activity into multiple concurrent flows. It has one incoming edge and several outgoing edges. When data arrives at a fork node, it is duplicated for each outgoing edge. For example, you can use a fork node to indicate that when a new person is hired, actions are initiated by Human Resources, the IT Department, and Facilities Management. All these actions execute concurrently and terminate independently.

You show a fork node as a vertical line, with one incoming edge and several outgoing edges. Figure 9-22 is an activity diagram that models hiring a new employee.

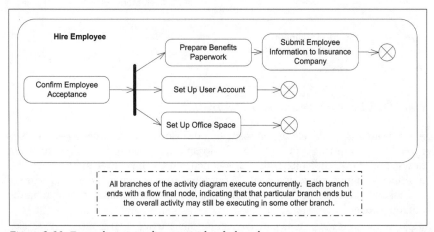

Figure 9-22. Example activity diagram with a fork node

A *join node* is effectively the opposite of a fork node; it synchronizes multiple flows of an activity back to a single flow of execution. A join node has multiple incoming edges and one outgoing edge. Once all the incoming edges have tokens, the tokens are sent over the outgoing edge.

You show a join node as a vertical line, with multiple incoming edges and one outgoing edge. Figure 9-23 is an activity diagram that models serving a meal.

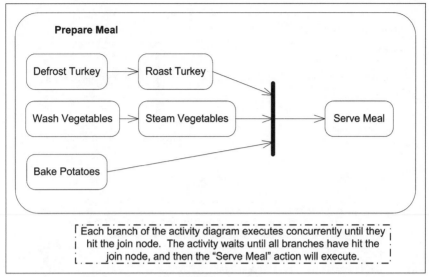

Figure 9-23. Example activity diagram with a join node

It is worth noting that activity diagrams don't have the advanced time-modeling notations that interaction diagrams have. So, while it's possible to show how to prepare a meal and serve everything at the same time with an activity diagram, you can't capture the time needed to cook each part of the meal. However, you can capture this information with a timing interaction diagram. See Chapter 10 for more information on interaction diagrams.

You can specify a boolean condition to indicate under what conditions the join node will emit a token allowing the flow to continue along its single output edge. This expression is called a *join specification* and can use the names of incoming edges and tokens arriving over those edges in the condition. You write a join specification near the join node inside of braces ({}). Figure 9-24 adds greeting guests to the steps involved in preparing a meal and ensures that you don't serve the meal until all the guests have arrived.

Final nodes

Two types of final nodes are used in activity diagrams: *activity final* and *flow final*. Activity final nodes terminate the entire activity. Any tokens that arrive at the activity final node are destroyed, and any execution in any other node is terminated, without results. You can have multiple activity final nodes in a single activity diagram, but a token hitting any of them terminates the whole activity. You show an activity final node as a black dot with a circle around it, as shown in Figure 9-4.

Flow final nodes terminate a path through an activity diagram, but not the entire activity. Flow final nodes are used when the flow of an activity forks, and one

Activity
Diagrams

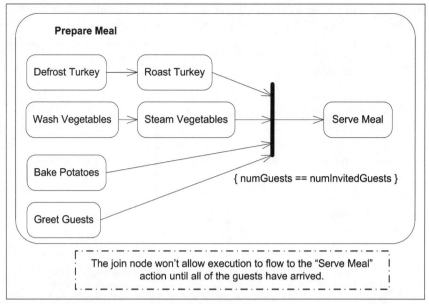

Figure 9-24. Join node with a join specification

branch of the fork should be stopped but the others may continue. Show a flow final node as a circle with an X in it, as shown in Figure 9-22.

Advanced Activity Modeling

UML 2.0 introduces several powerful modeling notations for activity diagrams that allow you to capture complicated behaviors. Much of this new notation is clearly targeted at moving closer to executable models, with things such as executable regions and exception handling. While not all the notations described in this section are used in every model, these constructs are invaluable when applied correctly.

Activity Partitions

There are times when it is helpful to indicate who (or what) is responsible for a set of actions in an activity diagram. For example, if you are modeling a business process, you can divide an activity diagram by the office or employee responsible for a set of actions. If you are modeling an application, you may want to split an activity diagram based on which tier handles which action. You split an activity diagram using an *activity partition*. Show an activity partition with two parallel lines, either horizontal or vertical, called *swimlanes*, with the name of the partition in a box at one end. Place all nodes that execute within the partition between the two lines. Figure 9-25 shows an activity diagram partitioned by business unit.

There are times when trying to draw a straight line through your activity diagram may not be possible. You can show that a node is part of a partition by writing the partition name in parentheses above the name of the node. If the activities within

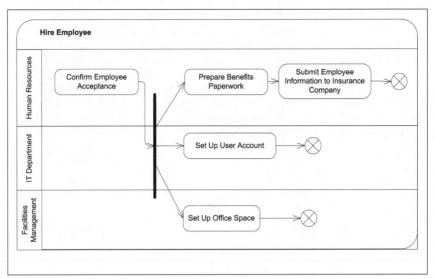

Figure 9-25. Activity diagram divided into partitions

a partition occur outside the scope of your model, you can label a partition with the keyword «external». This is frequently used when performing business modeling using activity diagrams. If the behavior being modeled is handled by someone external to your business process, you can mark the functionality with an external partition. Figure 9-26 shows examples of naming partitions directly on the node and using external partitions.

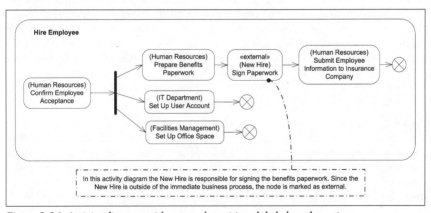

Figure 9-26. Activity diagram with external partitions labeled on the actions

A partition has no effect on the data flow in an activity, however depending on the entity represented by the partition, there are implications on how actions are handled. If a partition represents a UML classifier, any method invocation within that partition must be handled by an instance of that classifier. If the partition represents an instance, the same restrictions apply, except that behaviors must be handled by the specific instance referenced by the partition. For example, if you

Activity
Diagrams

are modeling a system that has a partition named LoginService, all actions performed within that partition should be handled by an instance of your LoginService. However, if you have a partition that represents an instance of a User class named CurrentUser, all actions in that partition must be handled by the CurrentUser instance. To indicate that a partition represents a class, you use the keyword «class» before the type name. Though the UML doesn't explicitly state it, it is customary to show that a partition represents an instance by underlining the type name. Figure 9-27 shows an example of a partition representing a classifier and a partition representing an instance.

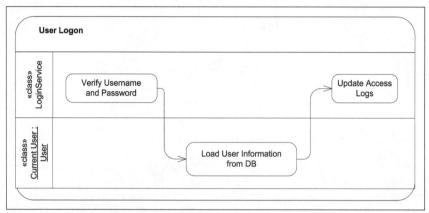

Figure 9-27. Activity diagram with partitions representing classes and instances

Partitions can also represent attributes with specific values. For example, you can have an activity diagram, which shows that at a certain point in its execution, an attribute has a specific value. You can use a partition to indicate the attribute and value available to actions executing within that partition. Indicate that a partition represents an attribute by placing the keyword «attribute», followed by the name of the attribute in a box above the value boxes. Figure 9-28 is an example of an activity diagram in which the UserRole attribute is specified to indicate what level of access a user needs to perform the given actions.

You can combine partitions to show arbitrarily complex constraints on an activity diagram. For example, you can have two partitions that indicate the business department responsible for particular functionality and two partitions indicating the geographic location of the departments. These are called *multidimensional partitions* and are new to UML 2.0. You can show a multidimensional partition by using both horizontal and vertical intersecting partitions, as shown in Figure 9-29.

Exception Handling

UML 2.0 activity diagrams provide support for modeling exception handling. An exception is an error condition that occurs during the execution of an activity. An exception is said to be *thrown* by the source of the error and *caught* when it is handled. You can specify that an action can catch an exception by defining an *exception handler*. The exception handler defines the type of exception, and a behavior to execute when that particular exception is caught.

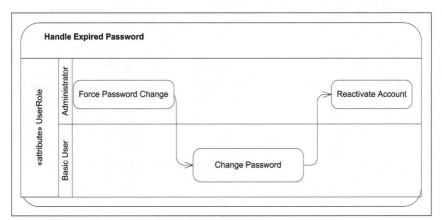

Figure 9-28. Simple attribute partition example

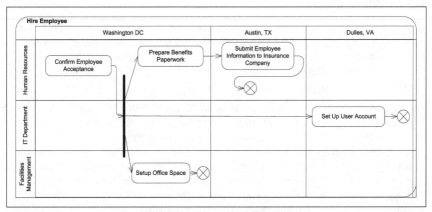

Figure 9-29. Activity diagram with multidimensional partitions

You show an exception handler as a regular node with a small square on its boundary. Draw a lightning-bolt-style edge from the protected node to the small square. Finally, label the edge with the type of the exception caught by this handler. Figure 9-30 shows an example exception handler.

If an exception occurs while an action is executing, the execution is abandoned and there is no output from the action. If the action has an *exception handler*, the handler is executed with the exception information. When the exception handler executes, its output is available to the next action after the protected node, as though the protected node had finished execution.

If the action doesn't have an exception handler, the exception propagates to outer nodes until it encounters an exception handler. As the exception leaves a node (an action, structured activity node, or activity) all processing in the node is terminated. It is unspecified what happens if the exception makes it to the top level of a system without being caught; UML 2.0 profiles can define specific behavior to handle this.

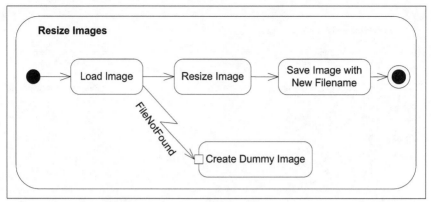

Figure 9-30. Activity diagram with an exception handler

Expansion Regions

You can show that an action, or set of actions, executes over a collection of input data by placing the actions in an *expansion region*. For example, if you had an action named Check Out Books that checked each of the provided books out of a library, you can model the checkout book action using an expansion region, with a collection of books as input.

You show an expansion region using a dashed rectangle, with rounded corners surrounding the actions that should execute for each piece of input data. Place a row of four input pins on the dashed boundary to represent a collection of data coming into the region. You show a line with an arrow to the row of input pins, and then from the input pins to the input pin of the first internal action. Likewise, you show a row of four output pins on the dashed boundary, with edges coming from the last action's output pin to the row of four output pins on the region. Figure 9-31 shows the Check Out Book expansion region.

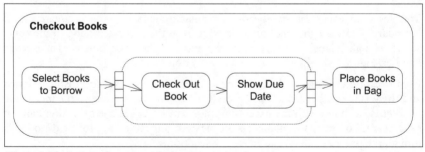

Figure 9-31. Activity diagram with an expansion region

The use of four input pins simply represents a collection of input data; it doesn't specify how much data is actually presented to the expansion region. The region executes for each piece of data in the collection and, assuming there are no errors, offers one piece of output data from each execution.

You can use the keywords «parallel», «iterative», or «stream» to indicate if the executions of the expansion region can occur concurrently (parallel), sequentially (iterative), or continuously (stream). Place the keyword in the upper left of the expansion region. Figure 9-32 shows a video encoder that streams the frames through the various stages of encoding as soon as they are available.

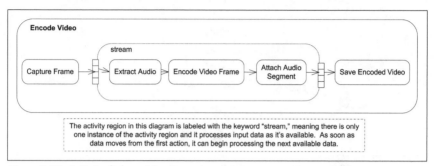

Figure 9-32. Activity dialog with a streaming region

Looping

UML 2.0 defines a construct to model looping in activity diagrams. A *loop node* has three subregions: setup, body, and test. The test subregion may be evaluated before or after the body subregion. The setup subregion executes only once, when first entering the loop; the test and body sections execute each time through the loop until the test subregion evaluates to false.

The specification gives no suggested notation for loop nodes, however you can improvise one using activity regions. Conceptually, a loop node looks like Figure 9-33.

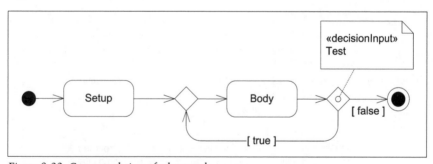

Figure 9-33. Conceptual view of a loop node

Using activity partitions, you can express this as a single node, as shown in Figure 9-34.

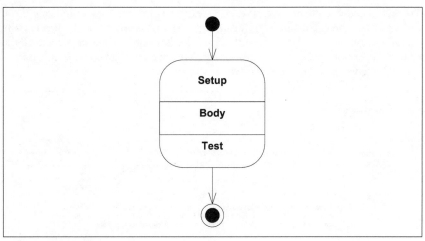

Figure 9-34. A sample looping node notation

Streaming

An action is said to be *streaming* if it can produce output while it is processing input. For example, an action representing a compression algorithm can take audio input data from a streamed input and send compressed audio along a streamed output.

You indicate that an action is streaming its input and output by placing the keyword stream in braces ({}) near the edges coming in and out of an action. Figure 9-35 shows an example audio encoding that is streaming data.

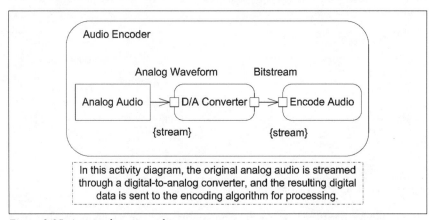

Figure 9-35. Activity diagram with streaming actions

UML provides a shorthand notation for streaming edges, and input and output pins: use a solid arrowhead or rectangle. Figure 9-36 shows the same audio encoder, but is drawn using the streaming shorthand notation.

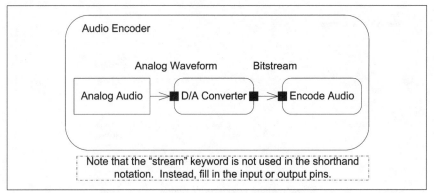

Figure 9-36. Activity diagram with streaming actions using shorthand notation

The UML specification expects that vendors will provide base classes for domain-specific activities users can employ to model an application-specific problem. You may also mark a set of actions as streaming using an expansion region. See "Expansion Regions" for more information.

Interruptible Activity Regions

You can mark that a region of your activity diagram can support termination of the tokens and processing by marking it as an *interruptible activity region*. For example, you may want to make a potentially long-running database query as interruptible so that the user can terminate things if he doesn't want to wait for the results.

You indicate a region is interruptible by surrounding the relevant nodes with a dashed rectangle that has rounded corners. You indicate how the region can be interrupted by drawing a lightning-bolt-style edge leaving the region and connecting to the node that assumes execution. If a token leaves the region over this edge, all other processing and tokens inside the region are terminated. The token leaving the region is unaffected.

Typically the source of an interruption is the receipt of a signal from an external entity. You show receipt of a signal as a concave pentagon, with the name of the signal inside. Figure 9-37 shows an example of a long-running database query being interrupted by user input.

Central Buffer Nodes

UML 2.0 introduced a new type of activity node, called the *central buffer node*, that provides a place to specify queuing functionality for data passing between object nodes. A central buffer node takes inputs from several object node sources and offers them along several object node outputs. For example, there may be two car-manufacturing plants feeding a car dealer supply line. A central buffer node can be placed between the manufacturing plants and the dealers to specify prioritization of deliveries or sorting of the manufactured cars. You show a central buffer node as a rectangle with the keyword «centralBuffer» at the top and the

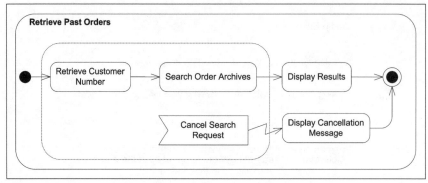

Figure 9-37. Activity diagram with an interruptible region

type of object written in the center. Figure 9-38 shows an example central buffer node feeding car dealer supply lines.

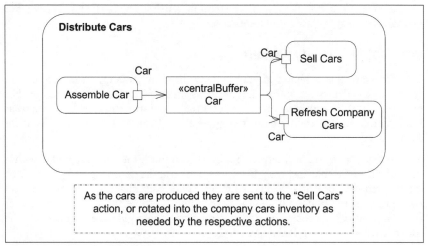

Figure 9-38. Activity diagram with a central buffer node

Data Store Nodes

A *data store node* is a special type of central buffer node that copies all data that passes through it. For example, you can insert a data store node in your activity diagram to indicate that all interactions are logged to an external database, or that when an article is submitted for review, it is automatically stored in a searchable archive.

You show a data store node as a stereotyped version of an object node. Show the node as a rectangle, and place the keyword «datastore» above the name of the node. Figure 9-39 shows a data store node.

If the same object passes through a data store node, the specification states that the previous version of the object will be overwritten.

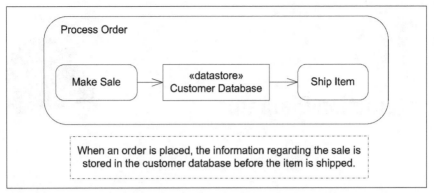

Figure 9-39. Activity diagram with a data store node

You can show transitions from a data store node that have additional information to select a subset of the data stored in a data store node, similar to a database query. The specification doesn't require any particular syntax and suggests showing the selection criteria in a note labeled with the keyword «selection». Figure 9-40 shows an activity diagram that uses a data store node to send welcome packets to new customers.

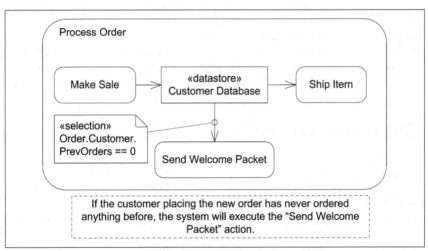

Figure 9-40. Activity diagram with a data store selection

10

Interaction Diagrams

A fundamental goal of UML 2.0 is to allow users to capture more than just structural relationships. UML 2.0 is intended to capture processes and flows of events. Interaction diagrams draw from nearly every other facet of the language to put together a set of diagrams that capture communications between objects. UML 2.0 has greatly expanded UML 1.x's ability to describe complex flow of control; one of the largest sections of the UML 2.0 specification is the interaction diagrams section. Because of the expanded functionality, quite a bit of new terminology has been introduced. We'll cover all the terms in this chapter and try to give you a feel for what terms are really critical and which are there to formalize the specification.

What Are Interactions?

Interaction diagrams are defined by UML to emphasize the communication between objects, not the data manipulation associated with that communication. Interaction diagrams focus on specific messages between objects and how these messages come together to realize functionality. While composite structures show what objects fit together to fulfill a particular requirement, interaction diagrams show exactly *how* those objects will realize it.

Interaction diagrams are typically owned by elements in the system. For example, you may have an interaction diagram associated with a subsystem that shows how the subsystem realizes a service it offers on its public interface. The most common way of associating an interaction diagram with an element is to reference the interaction diagram in a note attached to the element.

You can show the details of an interaction using several different notations; however sequence diagrams are by far the most common. Other notations include interaction overviews, communication diagrams, timing diagrams, and interaction tables. Because sequence diagrams are used most frequently, each concept is introduced using that notation. The other notations are described in detail later in the chapter. The basic symbol for an interaction diagram is a rectangle with the keyword sd and the name of the interaction in a pentagon in the upper-left corner.

Figure 10-1 shows an example sequence diagram. The various parts of this diagram are explained throughout the chapter.

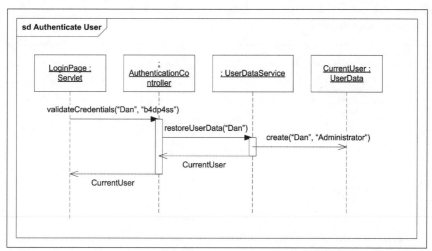

Figure 10-1. A sample sequence diagram

Interaction Participants

You show participants in an interaction using a rectangle called a *lifeline*. The term *lifeline* illustrates UML's bias toward representing interaction diagrams using the sequence diagram notation. When shown in sequence diagrams, participants have a dashed line dropping down from a rectangle that shows how long the object is actually in existence. When used in other interaction diagram notations, such as communication diagrams, a lifeline is simply a rectangle. You show the name of the participant in the rectangle using the following notation:

> object_name [selector] : class_name ref decomposition

where:

object_name
> Specifies the name of the *instance* involved in the interaction.

selector
> Is an optional part of the name that can identify which particular instance in a multivalued element is to be used (for example, which EventHandler in an array of EventHandlers).

class_name
> Is the name of the type of this participant.

decomposition
> Is an optional part of the name that can point to another interaction diagram that shows details of how this participant processes the messages it receives (see "Decomposition").

UML defines a reserved participant name, self, that indicates the participant is the classifier that owns this interaction diagram.

Figure 10-2 shows a trivial interaction diagram with two participants and a message between them.

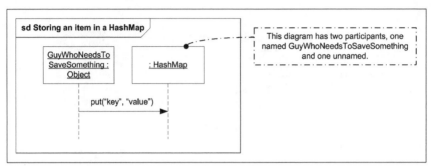

Figure 10-2. A trivial sequence diagram with two participants

You can show the destruction of a participant during an interaction using a stop symbol. Typically this is preceded by a «destroy» message to the object, though that isn't strictly necessary. Place an X at the bottom of the lifeline where the object ceases to exist. Figure 10-3 shows destroying a helper class after it has finished its work.

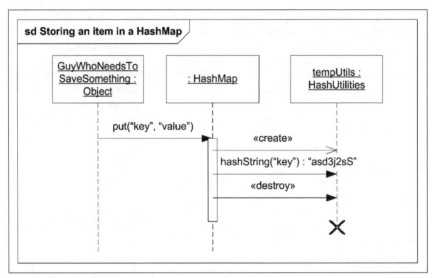

Figure 10-3. The destruction of a participant

To help make your sequence diagram accurately capture the behavior you are trying to model, you can introduce local variables. Local variables can hold return values, loop information, or just data you need for later processing. You show the values of local attributes relevant to the interaction using the same attribute syntax used inside of classifiers (see Chapter 2). Place their name and values in the upper left of the diagram, or in a note attached to the diagram. Figure 10-4 shows a more detailed version of the HashMap interaction using local variables.

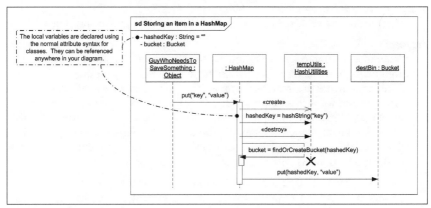

Figure 10-4. A more complete HashMap interaction using local variables

In addition to local variables, sequence diagrams can access data in the participants. See "Messages" for examples.

Messages

The focus of interaction diagrams is on the communication between lifelines. This communication can take many different forms: method calls, sending a signal, creating an instance, destroying an object, etc., all of which are collectively called *messages*. A message specifies the kind of communication, its sender, and its receiver. For example, a PoliceOfficer class instantiating a SpeedingTicket class is represented as a message from an instance of PoliceOfficer to the newly created instance of SpeedingTicket.

The most common use of messages is to represent method calls between two objects. When messages are used to indicate a method call, you can show the parameters passed to the method in the message syntax. The parameters should be one of the following:

- Attributes of the sending object
- Constants
- Symbolic values (expressions showing what the legal values can be)
- Explicit parameters of the enclosing interaction
- Attributes of the class owning the enclosing interaction

The syntax for a message is:

attribute = signal_or_operation_name (arguments) : return_value

where:

attribute

Is an optional part of the syntax that provides a shorthand way of showing that the return value from this message is stored in the specified attribute.

The attribute must be an attribute of the lifeline sending the message, a global attribute of the interaction, or an attribute of the class owning the interaction.

signal_or_operation_name
Specifies the name of the operation to invoke or the signal being emitted.

arguments
A comma-separated list of arguments to pass to the operation or signal. The arguments may be values or parameter names. If only argument values are used, arguments are matched against the operation or signal signature, in order. If you want to skip an argument, place a dash (-) where the argument would be. Skipped arguments have unknown values. You can explicitly identify a parameter name by following the text name with a colon (:) and then the value. If you use parameter names, you can omit arguments not relevant to the interaction. As with a dash, skipped arguments have unknown values.

You can prefix an argument with the keyword out or inout to indicate the argument is used to return a value. If the argument is used as an out argument, a value after the colon in the argument specification is interpreted to be the return value.

return_value
Explicitly states what the return value from this message will be.

Message notation varies based on the specific notation you use to show the details of the interaction. Because the most common representation of interactions is with sequence diagrams, you use the notation that's common with such diagrams. See the specifics about other notations in "Alternate Interaction Notations."

When using sequence diagram notation, you show a message as a solid line pointing from the sender's lifeline to the receiver's lifeline. If the message is an asynchronous message (meaning the caller doesn't block waiting for the receiver to process the message), you place an open arrowhead on the receiver's end of the line. Figure 10-5 shows an example of an asynchronous message.

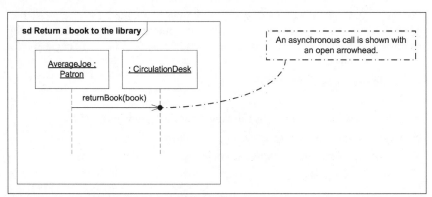

Figure 10-5. An asynchronous message between objects

When returning a book to the library, you typically don't wait around for the librarian to return the book to the shelves. Instead, you drop the book off at the

Circulation Desk and continue on your way. The open arrowhead indicates that the caller (AverageJoe) doesn't wait for any response from the CirculationDesk.

Because asynchronous messages don't require the sender to wait for a message to be delivered, depending on the transport mechanism, asynchronous messages can arrive out of order. For example, two network packets can take different routes to the same destination, with the second arriving before the first. You can show out-of-order reception by having the first message point to a spot below the reception point of the second message, as shown in Figure 10-6.

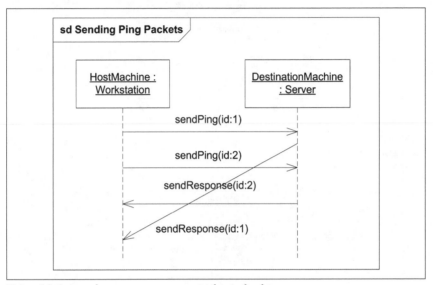

Figure 10-6. Asynchronous messages received out of order

In this example HostMachine sends two ping packets to DestinationMachine. Because of network differences in the routes taken, the response to the second ping arrives before the response to the first ping.

If a message represents synchronous communication (typically a method call), you place a filled arrow head on the receiver's end. You can show return values from a method using a dashed line with an open arrowhead pointing back to the caller. Figure 10-7 shows a method call to order an item and a confirmation number sent back as a return value.

If a message represents object creation, you show a dashed line, with an open arrow pointing to the newly created object's lifeline. By convention, the message is typically labeled with some variation of create. If there are no arguments to the message, you can simply label the message with the keyword «create», as in Figure 10-3. If there are arguments, you show them as parameters to a create( ) message. If there is a particular reason to show the creation message using a different label (such as a factory method), you should use that. Figure 10-8 shows an example that creates an instance of the class UserAccount.

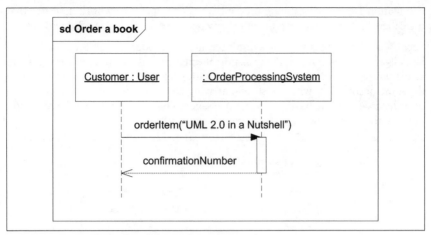

Figure 10-7. A method call and the resulting return value

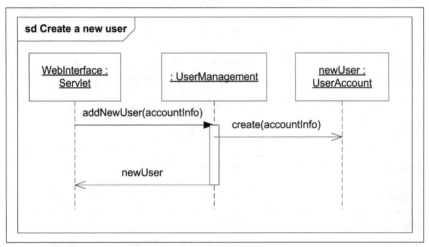

Figure 10-8. Showing object instantiation

Although this technique isn't mentioned in the specification, some modelers prefer to lower the rectangle representing the object to the end of the message line to clearly indicate the object didn't exist before this creation event. The advantage of this notation is that it clearly shows when the object comes into existence; the disadvantage is that you can't skim the top row and view the participants. Figure 10-9 shows the same diagram but lowers the newly created object.

UML defines two special types of messages: *lost messages* and *found messages*. Lost messages are messages that are sent but never reach their destination. Found messages are messages that are received by an object but the sender is unknown. For example, if you want to model an exception-handling mechanism, the sending of the exception is really irrelevant to the mechanism itself, so you can model that as a found message. Understand that unknown senders and receivers are relative concepts. The sender or receiver of a message may be unknown *as far as a*

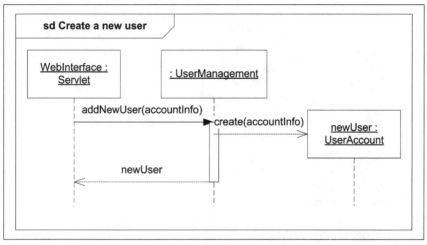

Figure 10-9. Object instantiation with the object lined up with the creation message

particular interaction is concerned, meaning it's really outside the scope of what you are trying to show, not that the message necessarily vanishes from existence (though that's permissible too).

You show a found message by starting the message from a black circle rather than the sender's lifeline. Figure 10-10 shows an example of a found message. The CircuitBreaker doesn't care where the power surge came from; it must terminate the power in all conditions.

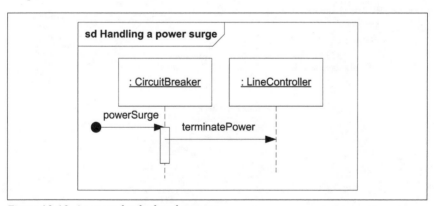

Figure 10-10. An example of a found message

Similarly, you show a lost message by terminating the message arrow at a black circle rather than a receiver's lifeline. Figure 10-11 shows a Workstation sending out a ping message that for some reason, (network failure) isn't received.

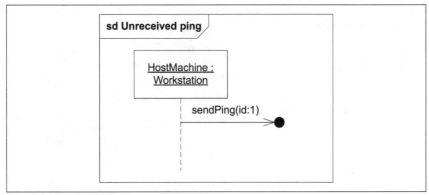

Figure 10-11. An example message being lost

Execution Occurrences

You can show an object is involved in executing some type of action (typically a method call) for a measurable amount of time using an *execution occurrence*. Execution occurrences are shown as gray or white rectangles on a lifeline. In practice, it is common to hear execution occurrences called "focus of control," because they indicate that an object is busy (has the focus of the system) for some period of time. Figure 10-12 shows several execution occurrences in response to messages.

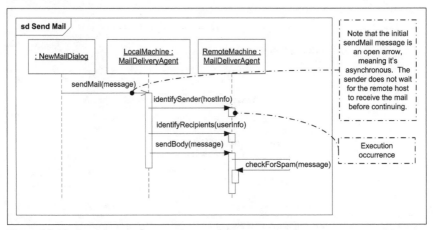

Figure 10-12. Several example execution occurrences

While not officially part of the specification, it was a common practice in UML 1.x to show messages starting from an execution occurrence on a lifeline to indicate that an object will send messages to other objects as part of processing a received message. With UML 2.0, it may be more appropriate to show a set of messages as an interaction fragment. Using interaction fragments, an appropriate interaction operator, and a reasonable name, you have much greater flexibility in expressing exactly how a piece of the system executes and how it fits into the bigger picture.

See "Combined Fragments" for more information on interaction fragments and the various ways you can organize messages to increase your diagram's readability.

State Invariants

UML allows you to place labels along a lifeline to convey conditions that must be true for the remainder of the interaction to be valid. These conditions are called *state invariants*. State invariants are typically boolean expressions, though they may be full UML states (see Chapter 8). For example, you may have a series of messages that initialize a participant. After the messages have completed, the participant must be in a well-known state for the remainder of the interaction to complete successfully. You can enforce that by placing a state invariant on your diagram after the initialization messages.

You show a boolean state invariant by simply placing the conditional inside curly braces ({}) on the lifeline of the object you want to check. The invariant will be evaluated after any messages that come above it on the diagram. Figure 10-13 shows a basic boolean invariant checking that an Account has been authenticated successfully.

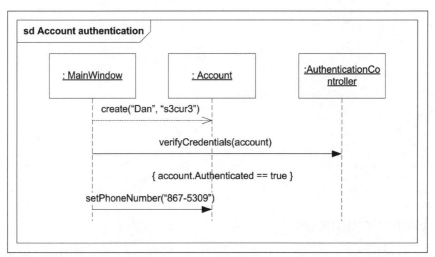

Figure 10-13. A state invariant ensuring that the account is in the proper state before continuing

You show an invariant as a UML state by simply drawing the state symbol (rectangle with rounded sides) over the appropriate part of the lifeline of the object you want to check. The actual information that is validated by the state can be expressed using the normal UML state diagram notation. Figure 10-14 shows the same Account authentication using a UML state.

UML allows you to place the state invariant information inside a note and link it back to the lifeline, though this doesn't tend to be as obvious to the reader as seeing a constraint directly on the lifeline in the proper sequence. Figure 10-15 shows a state invariant using a note.

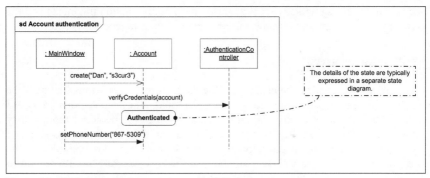

Figure 10-14. A state invariant using a real UML state

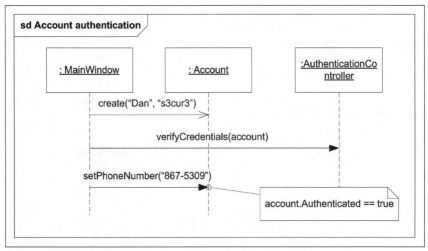

Figure 10-15. A state invariant using a note; authenticated must be true when setPhoneNumber is called

Event Occurrences

Event occurrences are the smallest building blocks of interaction diagrams; they represent moments in time when something happens. Sending and receiving a message are the most common types of event occurrences, though technically they can be any action associated with an object. For example, if object1 sends a message to object2, there are two event occurrences, a *message send* and a *message receive*. UML carefully defines interaction fragments as a set of event occurrences where ordering is significant because they represent events over time.

Each type of interaction diagram notation (sequence, communication, etc.) has a way of expressing the time-sensitive nature of the event occurrences. In a sequence diagram the event occurrences are ordered along the lifelines and are read from top to bottom. Figure 10-16 shows a sequence diagram with three of the event occurrences labeled (as mentioned earlier, any action associated with an object is an event occurrence, but to keep the diagram from getting out of control only three are labeled in the figure).

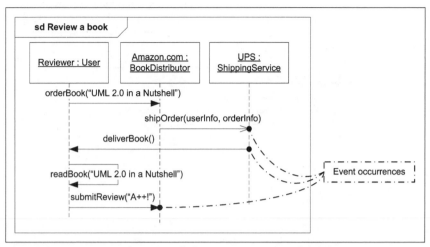

Figure 10-16. A sequence diagram with three event occurrences labeled

Traces

UML defines a *trace* as a sequence of event occurrences. The term *trace* is used when discussing sets of event occurrences and how they may be combined. Interaction diagrams allow you to combine fragments in such a way that the event occurrences are interleaved. This combined set of event occurrences is considered a new trace.

Throughout this chapter we will refer to a sequence of event occurrences as event occurrences rather than as a trace to try and reduce the number of keywords.

Combined Fragments

Often there are times when a particular sequence of event occurrences has special constraints or properties. For example, you may have a critical region within your interaction where a set of method calls must execute atomically, or a loop that iterates over a collection. UML calls these smaller pieces *interaction fragments*.

Interaction fragments by themselves aren't terribly interesting, however UML allows you to place them in a container called a *combined fragment* (it's called a combined fragment even if you have only one interaction fragment in there). Once they are placed in such a container, UML allows you to specify additional detail for each fragment, or how several fragments relate to each other.

Each combined fragment is made up of an *interaction operator* and one or more interaction fragments, which are the *interaction operands*. An interaction operator specifies how the interaction operands should be interpreted. The various interaction operators are described in detail later in this chapter.

As you do with full interactions, you show a combined fragment as a rectangle, with the interaction operator in a pentagon in the upper left and the interaction operands inside the rectangle. Figure 10-17 shows a combined fragment representing a critical section of code. The code must be executed atomically because of the interaction operand critical. This and other interaction operators are described in "Interaction Operators."

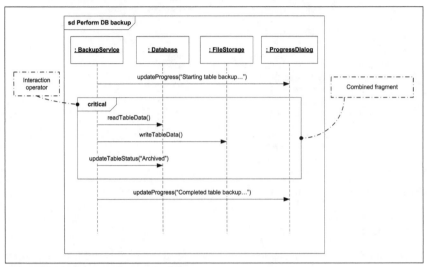

Figure 10-17. An example combined fragment

Depending on the interaction operator you choose for a combined fragment, you may need to specify multiple operands. You separate operands using a horizontal dashed line across the rectangle. Messages aren't permitted to cross between interaction fragments. The order of the operands is significant for some of the operators, so always read a combined fragment from top to bottom. See Figure 10-18 for an example of multiple operands.

Guard Conditions

An interaction fragment may have a guard condition that states when the fragment is valid (can be executed); as in an "if-then" condition. The syntax for a guard condition is simply:

[*boolean_expression*]

You show a guard condition directly above the first event occurrence in the relevant interaction fragment and on top of the associated lifeline. A guard condition can refer to any local data available to that lifeline, or to any global data available to the overall interaction; it can't refer to the local data of some other lifeline. Figure 10-18 shows an example of an alternative interaction operator that models an if-else condition.

See the description for each interaction operator to see when guard conditions are necessary and how they are used. If you don't place a guard condition before an interaction fragment, it is interpreted as a guard condition that always evaluates to true.

Interaction Operators

Each interaction operator defined in the UML 2.0 specification is explained in detail in the following sections. Each operator has an associated number of operands and a keyword that is placed in the pentagon of a combined fragment.

Alternatives

Alternates are a choice of the behavior that executes based on guard conditions placed before each operand. The interaction operator is alt. You may include an else guard condition that executes the associated operand when the other conditions are false. Figure 10-18 shows this.

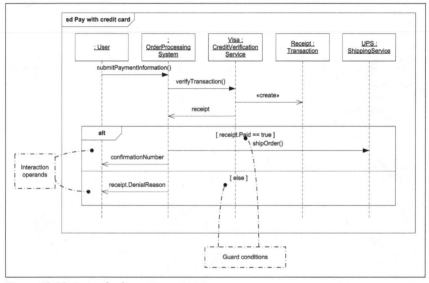

Figure 10-18. Example alternative operator

Option

Options are interaction fragments that executes only if the guard condition is true. The interaction operator is opt. Conceptually, options are similar to an alt operator with only one operand. Figure 10-19 shows an option operator.

Break

A *break* indicates that the associated interaction fragment operand should execute and then terminate the enclosing interaction. The interaction operator is break. A break is similar to the following code block:

```
if (guardCondition) { ... ; return; }
```

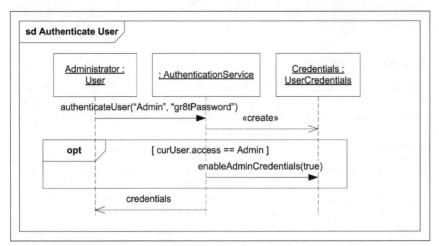

Figure 10-19. Example option operator

Figure 10-20 shows a break operator.

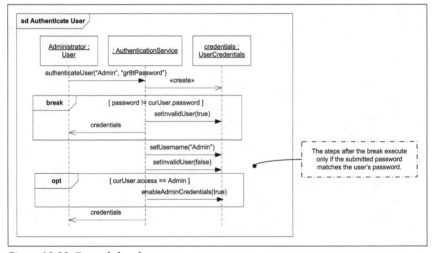

Figure 10-20. Example break operator

Parallel

Parallel indicates that the associated interaction fragments may be merged and executed in parallel. The interaction operator is par. UML specifies that the actual interleaving of the event occurrences of the operands must be done in such a way that the ordering in the original operand is maintained. For example, if the first operand consists of:

```
Step1
Step2
Step3
```

and the second consists of:

```
StepA
StepB
StepC
```

they can be merged into:

```
Step1
StepA
StepB
Step2
StepC
Step3
```

but not into:

```
Step1
StepB
Step2
StepA
Step3
StepC
```

because stepA and stepB would be executed out of order. Figure 10-21 shows an example of the parallel operator to model a desktop login sequence.

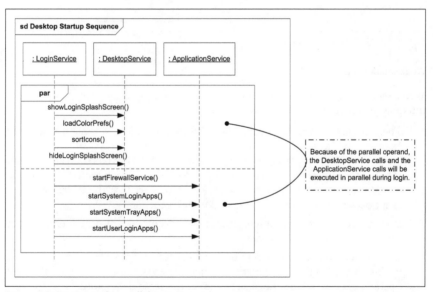

Figure 10-21. Example parallel operator

If you need to convey that a particular event occurrence *must* come before another event occurrence, UML has an explicit notation called a *general ordering*. You can show a general ordering anywhere in an interaction diagram, but it must connect two event occurrences. You simply draw a dotted line between the two event occurrences, with a solid arrow in the middle of the line pointing toward the occurrence that must happen second. For example, if you don't want the login splash screen in Figure 10-21 to be hidden until all the applications are started, you can indicate that the `startUserLoginApps()` call must occur before the `hideLoginSplashScreen()` call. Figure 10-22 shows how to use a general ordering to indicate that the application startup must complete first.

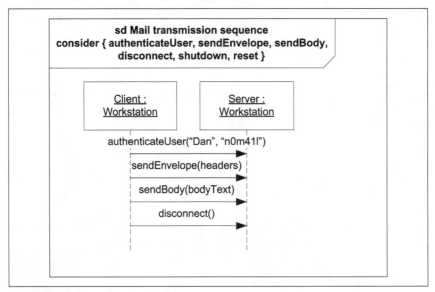

Figure 10-22. Example general ordering

Weak sequencing

Weak sequencing indicates that the event occurrences in each operand can be interleaved according to the following rules:

1. The ordering of the event occurrences within each operand is maintained. For example, if the first operand has <step1, step2, step3> and the second operand is <stepA, stepB, stepC>, they may be interleaved to <step1, stepA, step2, stepB, step3, stepC> because the order is maintained, but not to <step1, step3, stepA, step2, stepB, stepC> because the ordering of the event occurrences in the first operand is changed.

2. If event occurrences in different operands occur on different lifelines, they can be interleaved in any order.

3. If event occurrences in different operands occur on the same lifeline, they can be interleaved only in such a way that the event occurrences of the first operand execute before the occurrences of the second operand.

The interaction operator is seq. For Figure 10-22, a weak sequencing wouldn't change the way the calls are interleaved because the first operand has calls only to DesktopService and the second operand has calls only to the ApplicationService. However, if the sequence is changed so that the second operand includes a call to the DesktopService, it isn't allowed to execute until all the calls to DesktopService in the first operand are complete (Rule #3). Figure 10-23 shows this new sequence diagram.

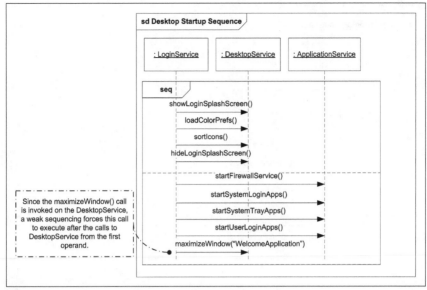

Figure 10-23. Example of a weak sequencing operator

Strict sequencing

Strict sequencing indicates that the ordering of the event occurrences is significant across lifelines, not just within the same lifeline (as with weak sequencing). The operands of a strict sequence must be executed in order, from top to bottom. The interaction operator is strict.

Negative

Negative indicates a set of event occurrences that are considered invalid, meaning the interaction can never execute this particular path. The interaction operator is neg. This particular operator is rarely used but can convey that the particular sequence isn't permitted. Figure 10-24 shows an example of an invalid call to a Graphics2D object. In this diagram, a UML note indicates to the reader why the particular sequence is invalid.

Critical region

A *critical region* indicates that the given event occurrences must be treated as an atomic block. The interaction operator is critical. Critical regions are typically used inside other interaction fragments (such as a parallel fragment) to ensure that a group of event occurrences can't be separated.

Figure 10-25 shows an example rendering engine loop that checks to see if map data is available for drawing. Because loading map data may be an expensive operation, we'll allow the loading to be executed in parallel with the rendering. However, compressed map data can't be rendered, so the loading and decompression must occur as an atomic operation.

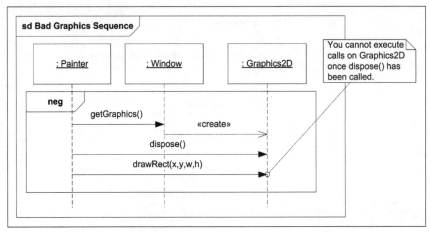

Figure 10-24. Example of a negative operator

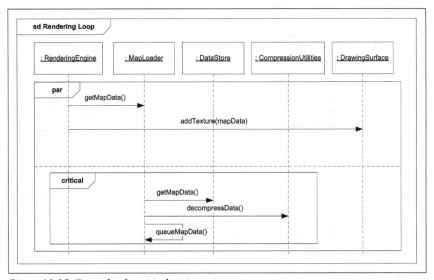

Figure 10-25. Example of a critical region operator

Because Figure 10-25 needs to represent a continuously running process (the rendering loop), it's better to model the looping conditions with the loop operator shown later in this chapter (see "Loop").

Ignore/consider

Ignore specifies a set of messages that aren't shown on the interaction fragment and can be safely ignored. This typically implies that the ignored messages are irrelevant for the purpose of the diagram; however, they may still occur during actual execution. The interaction operator is ignore, and the syntax is:

```
ignore { messagename, messagename, ... }
```

Figure 10-26 shows an example of the ignore operator that models a simple mail transmission protocol. In this sequence, ping and status messages are explicitly ignored. This means they can occur anywhere during this sequence and should be handled by the system, but are irrelevant to the flow of execution we're trying to model.

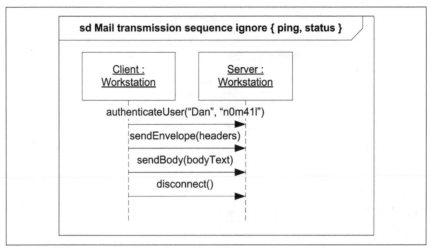

Figure 10-26. Example of an ignore operator

Consider specifies a set of messages that are explicitly relevant to the diagram, so you can safely ignore any other message. The interaction operator is consider, and the syntax is:

```
consider { messagename, messagename, ... }
```

Figure 10-27 shows the same mail transmission sequence as that shown in Figure 10-26 but explicitly considers authenticateUser, sendEnvelope, sendBody, disconnect, shutdown, and reset. Because shutdown and reset aren't shown on the sequence diagram, it's invalid for either message to occur during execution.

Assertion

An *assertion* indicates that the contained event occurrences are the only valid execution path. The interaction operator is assert. Assertions are typically combined with some kind of state invariant to enforce a state of a system.

Figure 10-28 shows a sequence diagram in which the user requests that maps be redrawn. The RenderingEngine instructs the DrawingSurface to remove all the existing textures, and the assertion guarantees there are no textures left.

Loop

A *loop* indicates that the contained event occurrences are to be executed some number of times. The interaction operator is loop. The notation for a loop includes a minimum and maximum number of times a loop should execute. You

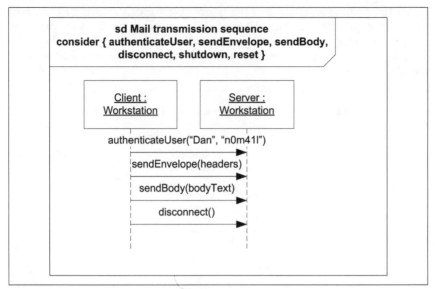

Figure 10-27. Example of a consider operator

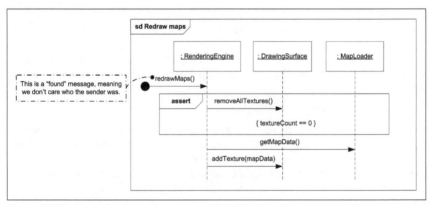

Figure 10-28. Example of an assertion operator

may also use a guard condition that is evaluated each time through the loop to terminate execution. The syntax for the operator is:

```
loop (min, max)
```

where both min and max are optional. If max is excluded, max equals min. max may be an asterisk (*) to indicate an infinite loop (or at least while the guard condition evaluates to true). If both min and max are excluded, min equals 0, and max equals infinity; in this case you likely want to have a guard condition to prevent the loop from executing indefinitely.

Figure 10-29 shows the rendering loop modeled in Figure 10-25. In this sequence diagram, the looping is explicitly shown with a guard condition that will terminate the loop when the user has set the quit flag to be true. There is also an inner loop that instructs the MapLoader to execute while there are maps to load.

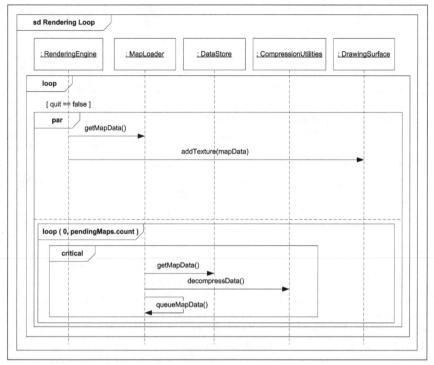

Figure 10-29. Example of a loop operator

Interaction Occurrences

An *interaction occurrence* is shorthand for copying one interaction into another, larger interaction. For example, you can create an interaction that simply shows user authentication and then reference it (create an interaction occurrence) in larger, more complete interaction diagrams.

The syntax for an interaction occurrence is a combined fragment rectangle with the interaction operator ref. Place the name of the referenced interaction in the rectangle. UML allows parameters to be passed to referenced interactions using the following syntax:

```
attribute_name = collaboration_occurrence.interaction_name ( arguments ) :
return_value
```

where:

attribute_name
   Is an optional part of the syntax that specifies what attribute the return value should be applied to. The attribute must be an attribute of a lifeline in the larger interaction.

collaboration_occurrence
   Is an optional scoping of the referenced interaction if it is part of a larger collaboration.

interaction_name
Is the name of the interaction to copy.

arguments
Is a comma-separated list of arguments to pass to the referenced interaction. The arguments may be values or parameter names. If only argument values are used, arguments are matched against the interaction parameters, in order. If you want to skip an argument, you place a dash (-) where the argument would be. Skipped arguments have unknown values. You may explicitly identify a parameter name by following its text name with a colon (:) and then the value. If you use parameter names, you may omit arguments not relevant to the interaction. As with a dash, skipped arguments have unknown values.

You may prefix an argument with the keyword out or inout to indicate that the argument is used to return a value. If the argument is used as an out argument, a value after the colon in the argument specification is interpreted to be the return value.

return_value
Is an optional part of the reference that, if present, indicates the value returned by the copied interaction.

Figure 10-30 shows a simple mail transmission sequence diagram that uses an interaction occurrence to refer to another sequence diagram that illustrates user authentication. In this example, the return value from the interaction occurrence is ignored, so it isn't assigned to any variable.

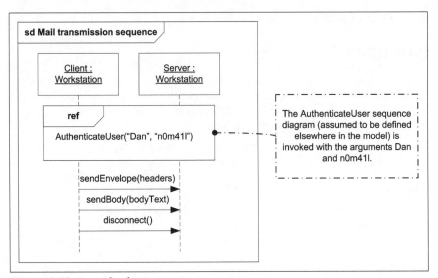

Figure 10-30. Example of an interaction occurrence

Decomposition

A participant in an interaction diagram may be a complex element in and of itself. UML allows you to link interaction diagrams by creating a *part decomposition* reference from a participant to a separate diagram. For example, you may have a Purchase Item interaction diagram that has a participant execute a credit card authorization. The actual details of the authorization process are probably not of interest to the readers of your Purchase Item diagram; however, they are vitally important to the developers responsible for the authorization subsystem. To help reduce clutter on your diagrams, you can create a separate diagram showing how the authorization subsystem validates credit cards and place a decomposition reference to that on the Purchase Item diagram.

To create a part decomposition reference, simply place ref interaction_diagram_ name after the instance name in the head of your lifeline. Figure 10-31 shows how the Purchase Item and authorization diagrams can be modeled.

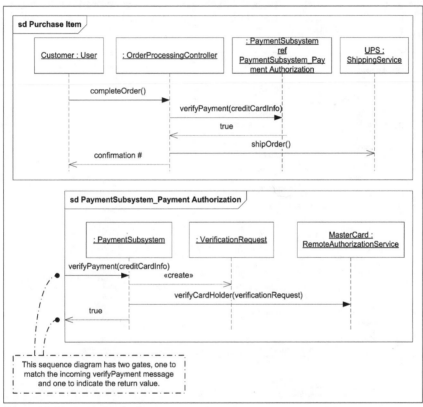

Figure 10-31. Example of a decomposition diagram

Messages that come into or out of the decomposed lifeline are treated as *gates* that must be matched by corresponding gates on the decomposition. A gate represents a point where a message crosses the boundary between the immediate interaction fragment and the outside environment. A gate has no symbol of its own; you simply show a message pointing to the edge of the frame of an interaction fragment. The entire purpose of a gate is to show an object that sent a message connecting to the object that received the message.

By default, a gate's name is based on the direction (in or out) and the message in question. For example, a gate showing a message named verifyPayment leaving an interaction fragment is named out_verifyPayment. However, you may explicitly name gates if that adds readability to your diagram.

If the messages shown in the decomposition are part of a combined fragment in the larger interaction diagram, the decomposition must inherit the same interaction operand. UML defines this as *extra-global*. For example, if the larger interaction is part of an assert interaction operand, and the state invariant is declared on the lifeline you want to decompose, that state invariant (and its assertion) must apply to your decomposition. You can show extra-global combined fragments by drawing the combined fragment on your decomposition, but making the combined fragment rectangle larger than your decomposition rectangle. Figure 10-32 shows an assertion decomposition of the rendering engine example used earlier in this chapter.

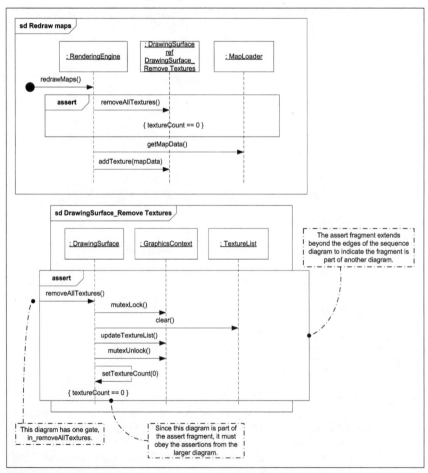

Figure 10-32. Example of a decomposition with extra-global fragments

The UML specification recommends that you name your decomposition diagrams using an abbreviation for the object being decomposed, followed by an underscore (_), followed by the name of the interaction. For example, if you are modeling a credit card authorization system and want to show how a card is validated, you can name your decomposition CCAS_Validation.

You can also show decompositions inline by showing parts of the decomposed element attached as smaller rectangles to the bottom of the head of the lifeline. Each part gets its own lifeline. This can be useful to show inner classes receiving or sending messages. For example, it is common practice in Java to declare an inner anonymous class to handle GUI events. If you felt this was relevant to your interaction you can show this level of detail on the main interaction diagram. However, inline notation is relatively uncommon because decompositions are typically used to show a complex, subinteraction that would clutter the top-level diagram.

Figure 10-33 shows an example inline part decomposition where MainWindow has two inner classes: an anonymous WindowListener and an instance of an EventHandler named mEventHldr.

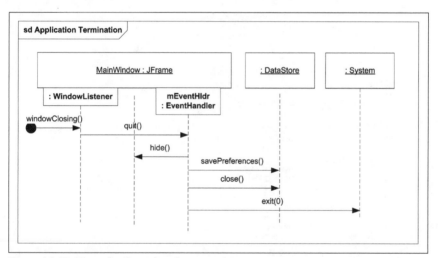

Figure 10-33. Example of an inline decomposition

Continuations

Typically used with interaction references, *continuations* allow you to define different branches of an alternative interaction outside of the alternative itself. Continuations are conceptually similar to named blocks of functionality.

The notation for continuations can be particularly confusing. You show a continuation using the symbol for states, a rectangle with rounded sides; however, the position of the rectangle changes the meaning of the diagram. You place a continuation at the *beginning* of an interaction to *define* the behavior for that continuation. You *use* a continuation by showing the rectangle at the *end* of an interaction. Finally, continuations with the same name must cover the same life-lines (and only those lifelines).

Figure 10-34 shows the first of three sequence diagrams demonstrating a continuation; this one displays the details of a Login sequence. After the password is retrieved from the database, an alternative interaction is entered. If the passwords match, various flags are set on the UserCredentials. After setting the flags, there is a continuation named Login success, in which users of this sequence diagram can plug in their own functionality. If the passwords don't match, the else part of the alternative interaction executes, which leads to the Login failed continuation. Notice the continuation symbols are at the *end* of each interaction operand, indicating this diagram uses an externally defined continuation.

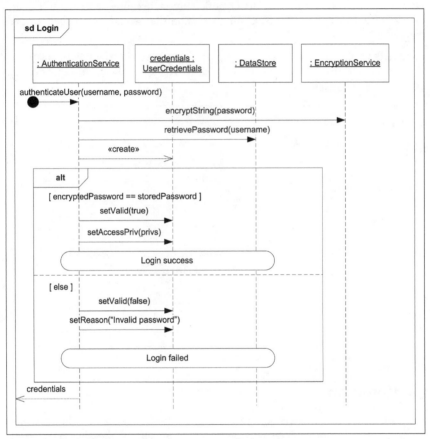

Figure 10-34. Using a continuation in a sequence diagram

Figure 10-35 shows the second diagram, a sequence diagram that makes use of the Login sequence and defines continuations for Login success and Login failed. If the correct password was entered, the Login success continuation is executed; otherwise, the Login failed continuation is run. Notice in this diagram that the continuation symbols are at the *top* of the interaction, indicating that this diagram defines the behavior to execute.

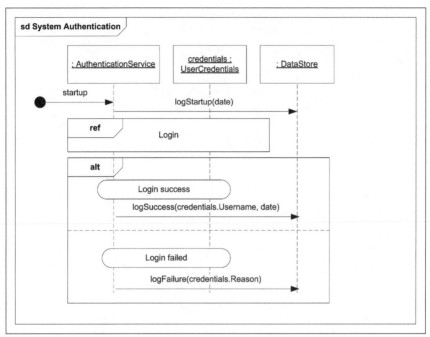

Figure 10-35. Defining continuations in a sequence diagram

Taken together, these two diagrams are equivalent to Figure 10-36.

Sequence Timing

UML provides a notation to capture a specific time associated with an event occurrence. You simply place a small horizontal line next to an event occurrence to capture the time of the occurrence, or place a timing constraint on it. Typically, you use a variable to capture a specific instance in time and then represent constraints as offsets from that time. Constraints are expressed like state invariants and placed next to the event occurrence.

For example, if you want to express that a credit card authorization system must return approval or denial within three seconds of placing the request, you can place time constraints on the event occurrence, as shown in Figure 10-37.

Alternate Interaction Notations

UML provides several notations for capturing interactions. The first part of this chapter used the sequence diagram notation. The remainder of this chapter describes the other notations available and when they may be more appropriate than sequence notation.

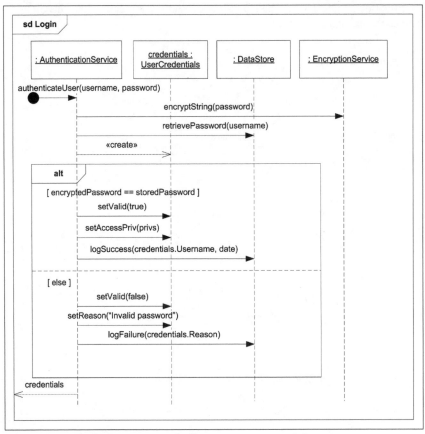

Figure 10-36. The final sequence, with all continuations expanded

Communication Diagrams

Communication diagrams allow you to focus on the elements involved in interactions rather than the detailed sequencing and flow control allowed in sequence diagrams. Most UML tools can automatically convert from a sequence diagram to a communication diagram; however, because communication diagrams aren't as expressive,.some information may be lost.

When you're modeling with communication diagrams, objects are represented by a rectangle, and connections between objects are shown as a solid line. Each message has a sequence number and a small arrow indicating the direction of the message along a given connection. Communication diagrams can't show message overtaking (see Figure 10-6 earlier in the chapter) or interaction fragments.

Figure 10-38 shows a simple sequence diagram and the equivalent communication diagram.

The syntax for a message name is:

    sequence_number: name [recurrence_or_guard]

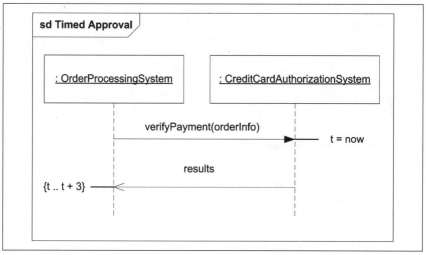

Figure 10-37. A sequence diagram with hard timing requirements

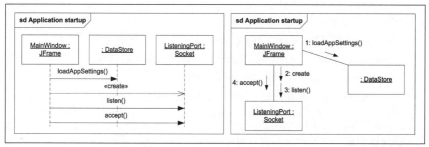

Figure 10-38. Example of a sequence diagram and its equivalent communication diagram

where:

sequence_number

> Is the index of the message with 1 being the index of the first message in the diagram. You show nested message calls by appending the original message number with a decimal and then starting a new sequence. For example, if the listen( ) call in Figure 10-38 makes a nested call to startTimer( ), number startTimer( ) as 3.1.

> You can show concurrent messages using letters in the sequencing. For example, if the ListentingPort instance can support multiple parallel listening calls, the MainWindow instance can call the listen( ) call twice, labeling the first call as 3a and the second as 3b. Both calls can execute concurrently.

name

> Is the name of the message being sent (or method call).

recurrence_or_guard

Is an optional part of the syntax that allows you to specify a boolean condition that must be true for the message to occur, or a range of integer values for looping. Guard conditions are represented as normal boolean expressions; for example, [password.Valid == true]. UML doesn't provide a syntax for specifying looping constraints but does say they must begin with an asterisk (*). For example, you can represent a loop that executes from 0 to 10 as *[i = 0 .. 10].

Interaction Overview Diagrams

Interaction overview diagrams represent interactions using a simplification of the activity diagram notation (see Chapter 9). Interaction overview diagrams can help you visualize the overall flow of control through a diagram; however, they don't show detailed message information.

You can embed interactions or interaction occurrences inside an interaction overview diagram if it is helpful to see message details for a subset of the overall interaction.

Several sequence diagram concepts are supported in interaction overview diagrams:

- Show combined fragments using a *decision node* and *merge node*.
- Show parallel interactions by using a *fork node* and *join node*.
- Show loops as cycles in the activity diagram.
- Show names of the lifelines involved in an interaction using the keyword lifelines after the name of the interaction overview diagram, followed by a comma-delimited list of each lifeline's name (including any colon separators that may or may not be part of the name).

Figure 10-39 is an interaction overview diagram showing a subset of the interaction shown in Figure 10-36.

Timing Diagrams

Timing diagrams are a special representation of interactions that focus on the specific timings of messages sent between objects. You can use timing diagrams to show detailed time constraints on messages or to show when changes occur within lifelines with respect to time. Timing diagrams are most often used with real-time or embedded systems.

Unlike sequence diagrams, timing diagrams are read left to right rather than top to bottom. You show a lifeline name along the left edge of the diagram. The various states of the lifeline are then listed, followed by a graphical representation of the transitions between these states. Figure 10-40 shows an example of a timing diagram in which the MailServer object progresses through several states.

In Figure 10-40, the MailServer starts in the Idle state until the Login event occurs. The Login event causes the MailServer to transition to Authenticated. When the sendMail event occurs, the MailServer transitions to Transmitting and remains there until disconnected.

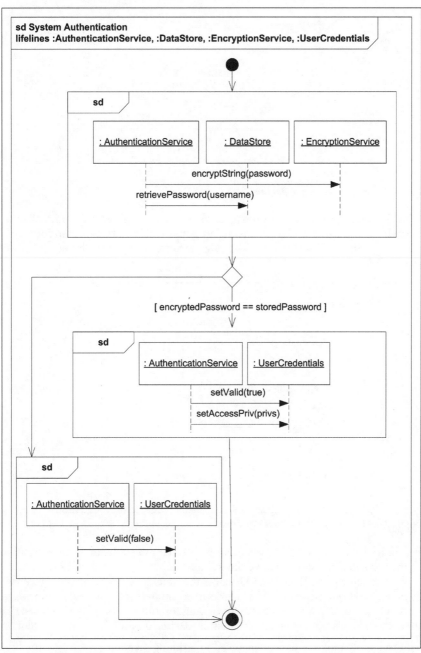

Figure 10-39. Example of an interaction overview diagram

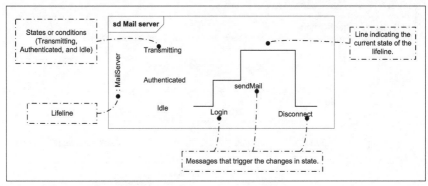

Figure 10-40. Simple timing diagram

When reading the diagram left to right, you can use the length of the timeline to indicate how long the object remains in a particular state. To associate time measurements, you show tick marks along the bottom part of the frame, as shown in Figure 10-41.

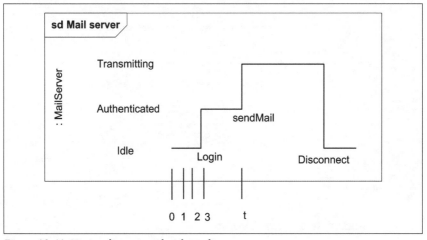

Figure 10-41. Timing diagram with tick marks

Figure 10-41 shows that the Login event is received three time units after the start of the sequence. To show relative times, you can mark a specific instance in time using a variable name. Figure 10-41 marks the time the sendMail event is received as time t. You can use relative time marks in constraints to indicate that a message must be received within a specified amount of time. Figure 10-42 shows the Disconnect message must be received within 10 time units of the sendMail event.

You can show multiple objects involved in a timing diagram by stacking the lifelines. You show messages between objects using an arrow from one timeline to another. The start and end of the arrow correspond to when the message is sent and received. This notation shows the triggers that cause a transition; however it

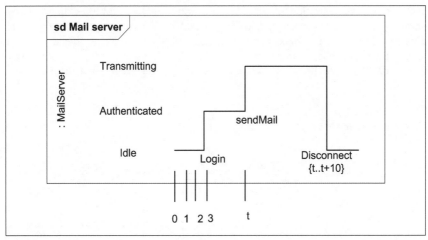

Figure 10-42. Timing diagram with time constraints

very quickly becomes unreadable if a lot of messages are exchanged. Figure 10-43 shows the MailServer talking with a client, Desktop.

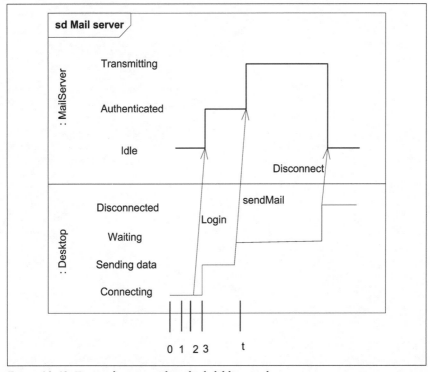

Figure 10-43. Timing diagram with multiple lifelines and messages

UML provides a variation on the timeline notation that simplifies diagrams by showing state names between two horizontal lines that cross when the state changes. This notation makes it much easier to show multiple objects along a single timeline, but it doesn't show the messages that trigger transitions. Figure 10-44 shows the MailServer and Client lifelines progressing through state transitions.

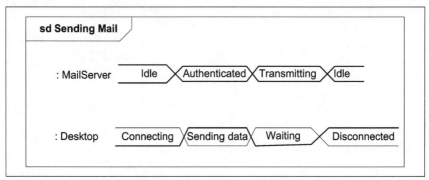

Figure 10-44. Timing diagram using a simpler timeline notation

11

Tagged Values, Stereotypes, and UML Profiles

The UML described in the previous chapters allows you to understand any UML model. You can understand the analysis of a billing system, the implementation model of a CORBA system, a gaming system in C++, or an EJB e-commerce system.

Practitioners rarely work on such diverse systems at one time, however, and no UML model will represent more than one type of application. More commonly, a practitioner (that's you) works with colleagues on one system or a series of closely related systems exclusively. For example, you might design a series of gaming systems, or a series of .Net systems. And, as you might expect, the specific concerns of a gaming system differ profoundly from those of a .Net system.

UML allows toolmakers to create a dialect called a *profile,* tailored to a specific niche. Within a niche, a *stereotype* gives specific roles to elements, and records additional context-specific information in *tagged values.* Profiles also include *constraints* that ensure integrity of use.

A practitioner familiar with a profile will immediately grasp the meaning of a model developed using that profile, because of the unique stereotypes. Moreover, the model contains deeper meaning, because of the tagged values, and the model has a higher degree of integrity, because of the constraints. This gives a distinct advantage to practitioners and tools working in the niche. People and tools unfamiliar with the profile will process it only at a formal level, without any special understanding.

Profiles are *the* standard mechanism to extend UML. The profile mechanism exists within UML so models applying a profile are fully UML compatible. This contrasts sharply with implementors' extensions in loosely specified languages such as C++, in which the specification allows inline assembler and #pragma statements, making it virtually impossible to port C++ programs between processors or between different compilers. A UML model applying a profile is UML, and any UML tool can process it.

Although a plethora of dialects can fragment the universality of UML, a dialect makes UML more useful. And isn't that what it's all about?

Modeling and UML in Context

Throughout the evolution of modeling, practitioners, implementors, academics, and other interested parties have found new and innovative ways to model, and new disciplines to model. It soon became apparent that the generality of the canonical UML was not concise enough for practitioners working full time in a particular language, technology, or platform, such as ANSII C++, Struts, or .Net. Moreover, practitioners in similar disciplines, such as process engineering, with different fundamental structures and constraints found UML interesting but not quite appropriate. They can better benefit from a UML-like language other than UML itself. Figure 11-1 illustrates this situation, where the Meta-Object Facility (MOF), explained more fully later in the chapter, comprises all UML models as well as UML-like models.

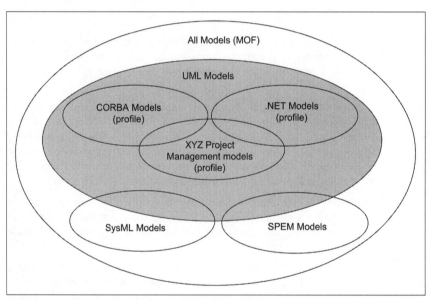

Figure 11-1. The universe of valid models in UML family

The authors of UML could have specialized UML for common programming languages (such as C++, C#, Java, and Visual Basic) and platforms (such as embedded systems, real-time operating systems (RTOS), EJB, and .NET). This would have created an unworkable modeling language, as each programming language or dialect polluted the specification with conflicting definitions. It would still require an extension mechanism because some "uncommon" language (such as Smalltalk) or new platform/technique or version (like EJB 3.0) would always be missing from the formal specification.

On the other hand, the authors could have stretched UML to greater abstraction to embrace uses other than software development, such as business modeling,

modeling the process of software development itself, or modeling systems engineering. This would have made everything even more abstract. Because designers work in only one specific domain, abstraction impedes concise expression, moving the models further from their domains.

Instead of burdening UML with complexity, or overwhelming it with abstraction, UML's authors factored out everything specific to domains and platforms. They created the profile extension mechanism to address the specific needs of specific application domains. CORBA models, for example, would be concise and precise, but would not influence a .Net model.

Although UML cousins, such as the Object Management Group's Software Process Engineering Metamodel (SPEM) and SysML.org's Systems Modeling Language (SysML), borrow much structure from UML, they also discard parts that bring no value to their disciplines. SPEM, best known as the basis for the Rational Unified Process (RUP), describes the process of software development in terms of process roles, work products, and activities. Between a software application and the process of software development, the fundamental structure and relationships between the parts change. Although much is similar in the state-chart, class, sequence, package, use case, and activity diagrams, for example, there is no implementation or component diagram, or interface. A profile specializing a few elements works, but it must exclude or constrain many basic concepts. MOF factors out the structure of UML itself for reuse in other disciplines. Using MOF, SPEM and SysML become metamodels at the same level as UML. UML remained close to the disciplines of general software development, and business and data modeling. In other disciplines, a new metamodel can be created from adding, dropping, and reorganizing UML packages to allow for a concise modeling of the discipline.

More formally, as seen in Figure 11-2, UML builds on its core infrastructure, MOF. MOF can be used by other modeling languages for other uses. The core UML can be used as is for building models directly, or it can be constrained by one or more profiles.

Each level is a level of abstraction. The levels are named M0, M1, M2, and M3, as they become more abstract. M0 is the concrete system—the code. M1 is the model of the system (of which M0 is just one realization)—the model where designers work. M2 is the language used to describe the model, in this case UML and, optionally, the profiles. M3, MOF, is the language used to describe UML and any similar modeling languages. MOF is far beyond the scope of this book. Suffice it to say, though, that MOF provides a formal infrastructure to UML, which explains why stereotypes resemble classes and components, and why tagged values resemble enumerations and attributes.

The M1 model, specifying your application, may have profiles associated with it. The architect determines the profiles to use according to the platform, language, and tools available. Deciding the profile effectively freezes the M2 layer. As an application modeler, you model classes, attributes, states, and all the other UML elements. You don't define new stereotypes or tagged values. You assign existing stereotypes. You fill in the values appropriate to the tags.

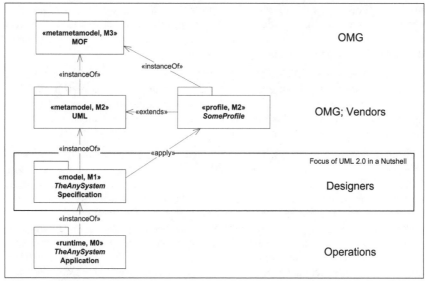

Figure 11-2. Layers of abstraction in UML

Unless you are also building your own tooling for code generation, reporting, and/or tracking, you will employ the profile(s) as is. As a «singleton», for example, the class needs certain supplementary information. The code generator needs the same questions answered for every «singleton»; no more, no fewer. It makes no sense to have a {multithread-safe=true} tagged value for one «singleton» if the code generator doesn't recognize it. If it does recognize it, every «singleton» should have it. It really depends on the tool.

Some teams do build their own tooling. Even then, only the toolsmith works in the M2 layer, and the modelers work in the M1 layer. Changes in the M2 layer must be conservative because one new tagged value in a stereotype can imply revisiting tens or hundreds of elements in the model. Changes in the M2 layer literally change the fundamental meaning of an M1 model. You've been warned.

Stereotypes

Stereotypes modify the intent of the elements to which they apply. They allow the differentiation of roles of an element within the model. For example, you can quickly differentiate classes stereotyped as *Controller* as having a different role in the system than those stereotyped as *View*.

Visually, UML allows graphical and textual representation of a stereotype. Graphics and text can be combined in various ways for node-type elements, as shown in Figure 11-3. The four elements that you see going across the top of the figure all represent the same combination of Form and key stereotypes but in different ways. Edge-type elements have only a textual representation, and thus you see «depends» on the dependency between Billing and Inventory.

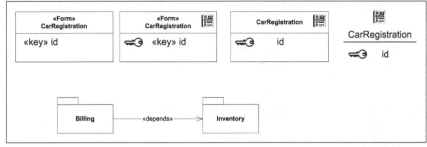

Figure 11-3. Various representations of stereotypes

When displayed as text, a stereotype is enclosed in guillemots («»), as in «MyStereotype». Because the guillemots require an extended character set to display correctly, you may also use double angle brackets to show a stereotype in 7-bit ASCII, as in <<MyStereotype>>.

Graphical icons are neither defined nor standardized by UML. You can expect toolmakers to extend the graphics differently, including coloring or shading, at their discretion. Avoid graphical symbols for interchange of models between different tools. However, within the controlled environment of a compatible set of tools, specialized graphics and/or colors will likely have more visual impact.

 While stereotypes have been around since the initial beta versions of UML, UML 2.0 has introduced significant changes to the 1.x versions:

- Elements may have zero, one, or more than one stereotype. The use and usefulness of stereotypes have become more and more evident. More toolmakers have incorporated them into their products. Modelers found it impossible to use otherwise complimentary tools because an element can have only one stereotype.

- Stereotypes may be nested. A specialized stereotype can build on the structure of a general stereotype. In the example provided later in this chapter, the EJBPrimaryKey stereotype extends the EJBCmpField stereotype, because all primary keys are ordinary fields as well.

- Tagged values are related through a stereotype rather than directly to the element. This avoids the possibility of name clashes with the introduction of multiple stereotypes per element.

You can tag an item in a UML model with more than one stereotype. Figure 11-4 shows multiple stereotypes as a list, with each stereotype enclosed in «guillemots».

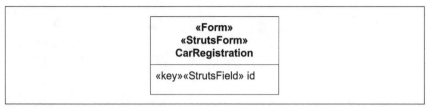

Figure 11-4. A class and an attribute, with two stereotypes each

Tagged Values

Having established an element's role within a system with a stereotype, the element likely needs information not available from the core UML, to fulfill its role. The stereotype defines a number of tagged values. Each tagged value is typed with a datatype—number, string, boolean, or user-defined enumeration. The upcoming section "UML Profiles" shows one way in which you might record, or define, the tagged values that you wish to include in a stereotype.

When you show them in a diagram, place the tagged values in a note element that is connected to the declaring element with a dashed line. Figure 11-5 shows the case of multiple stereotypes on one element. To keep the stereotypes and the corresponding tagged values clear, each stereotype is mentioned, and the tagged are values listed separately.

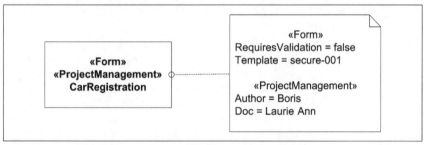

Figure 11-5. Tagged values shown classified by their owning stereotype

At first, you may confuse tagged values with attributes, but they exist at a different level of abstraction. Attributes, defined in the design model (M1), exist in the runtime system (M0). Tagged values, defined in the profile (M2), exist only in the design model (M1). The tagged values may provide hints to help the generation of code, either by human or machine. A tagged value of {optimize=space} will probably affect the code ultimately, although the actual value itself never appears in the code.

Constraints

Stereotypes give roles to elements. Tagged values provide role-specific information enriching the element in its role. While atomically the element knows its role and has all the information to fulfill it, the element must still interact with its neighbors. The element and their roles must be in harmony with the architectural vision. The element must also be internally consistent. Constraints (see "Constraints" in Chapter 2) provide the mechanism to specify rules for correct usage of the stereotyped elements.

UML Profiles

UML profiles combine the concepts of stereotypes, tagged values, and constraints to provide a coherent and concise dialect of UML for a specific family of applications. To make much use of a profile, some tooling must be provided. The application model drives code or application generation, so you have little or no control over the stereotypes, tagged values, or constraints comprising the profile. This section discusses the use of existing profiles (as opposed to defining your own).

Figure 11-6 depicts a partial UML profile defining a stereotype with its associated tagged values and a couple of constraints, as you might receive in a vendor's documentation. The profile extends classes with a stereotyped class, «EJBEntityBean». It extends attributes with two stereotyped attributes: «EJBPrimaryKey» and «EJBCmpField». It declares the respective tagged values for the stereotyped classes and attributes, and it declares the enumeration, TransactionIsolationLevel, to define the allowable values for the TransactionAttribute tagged value. The profile also adds the constraints that «EJBEntityBean» classes must have attributes of type «EJBCmpField» and «EJBPrimaryKey». Furthermore, attributes having these stereotypes can exist only in an «EJBEntityBean» class. From your point of view, the profile, along with its constituent stereotypes and tagged values, is read-only because it tells what the third-party tool expects in order to do its job.

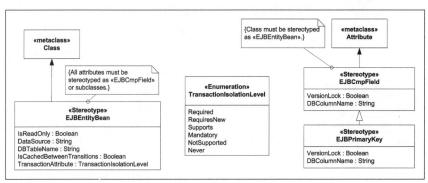

Figure 11-6. A partial specification UML profile

Figure 11-7 shows a portion of a model using the profile declared in Figure 11-6. Figure 11-8 indicates how the tagged value structures in the model relate back to the profile declaration. The notes containing the tagged values make the notation bulky if you need to show a set of tagged values for every class, attribute, operation, and relationship.

When aiming to expose the structure and relationships of a system, class diagrams rarely show tagged values. Referring again to Figure 11-7, one tiny class having two attributes becomes a constellation of four diagram elements. A modest class diagram of 10 classes can easily require 100 extra notes to show the tagged values, hopelessly confusing the diagram and destroying its impact. Instead, modelers often maintain the tagged values invisibly in the model, where tools can extract them as needed.

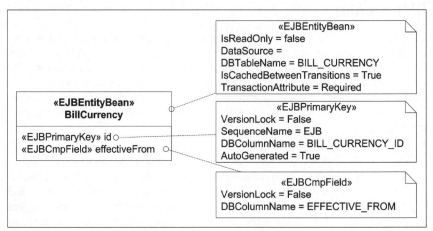

Figure 11-7. A stereotyped class and its stereotyped attributes, with their respective tagged values

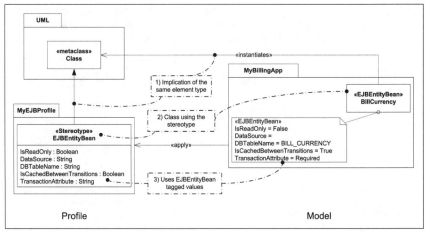

Figure 11-8. The partial specification UML profile, showing model elements applying it

The UML from the profile and the model is shown in Figure 11-8. This illustrates the relationships between the declarations of the profile and a conforming model. The stereotypes in the profile extend the concept of an element. In this case, the stereotype «EJBEntityBean» extends ordinary classes, as shown (1) by the implication of the same element type (metaclass), Class. In the models applying this profile, only classes may have that stereotype, as shown by the relationship (2). Having established that the BillCurrency is an «EJBEntityBean», it now has all the

«EJBEntityBean» tagged values, as shown by the relationship (3). Stereotypes that extend other stereotypes, as «EJBPrimaryKey» extends «EJBCmpField», have all the parent's tagged values. Ideally, tooling will aid, enforce, and validate by making available the correct tagged values and defaults according to the stereotype's definition. If not, the modeler must rely on discipline.

Tools and How They Use Profiles

UML tools use profiles to provide a spectrum of solutions. Tools providing Model-Driven Architecture (MDA) solutions have transformations from the Platform-Independent Model (PIM) to Platform-Specific Model (PSM) and from the PSM to the application. See Appendix A for a fuller discussion of MDA.

The OMG conceived the MDA as a vision rather than a specified method. Each vendor has a different, sometimes radically different, approach to MDA. Consequently, although the concepts of the PIM and the PSM vary greatly from one vendor to another, any one vendor's concept of the PIM and the PSM is strict and concrete. The extra roles and information, introduced as the PIM is refined to the PSM and the PSM to code, must be well defined and well controlled. Profiles provide the definition of the information to be captured and the constraints on a valid model. Each tool validates conformity to a profile in its own way. The PIM needs only one profile because it can be used and reused for different platforms. Each PSM, on the other hand, potentially needs a different profile because each specific platform has different issues and transformations to arrive at optimal code.

Tools previous to MDA still use profiles. In general, they provide a model-to-code code generation feature and often a code-to-model reverse engineering feature. To faithfully generate runnable code, many details must be stored in the model. Many language-dependent features can't be recorded in core UML. For example, UML doesn't recognize the Java keyword strictfp, which indicates floating-point processing. Without tagged values, a reverse-engineered system would not faithfully reproduce the same code when forward engineered.

12

Effective Diagramming

This chapter illustrates how you can create effective class diagrams. The diagrams presented in the reference section of this book have few elements. Those diagrams illustrate individual diagram elements, clear of any clutter; they aren't meant to illustrate diagram types. The diagrams in the reference section don't represent systems that you will encounter in real life. This final chapter illustrates some techniques you can use to make real-life diagrams convey your thoughts more effectively.

Wallpaper Diagrams

The classic novice class diagram displays all classes, attributes, operations, relationships, and dependencies for a system. As the number of classes grows, the diagram becomes huge and unmanageable. Imprudent reverse engineering drags in clutter. Figure 12-1 diagrams just a very small part of the Java Abstract Windowing Toolkit (AWT). You will not be able to read the diagram because it normally prints as an unwieldy nine pages. You're paying for the paper, so the diagram is shown here in a greatly condensed form.

Effective writers convey ideas through language constructs: sentences and paragraphs organize text, details reinforce ideas, and true but irrelevant facts are omitted. Modelers desiring to convey an idea—be it a structural overview, a pattern implementation, a detailed subsystem, or the detailed context of one class—must also use economy and focus. Figure 12-1 has neither economy nor focus. The diagram throws a mass of insignificant detail at readers, leaving the burden of understanding on them. It is a false economy to think that one diagram can present all the information of a multidimensional model.

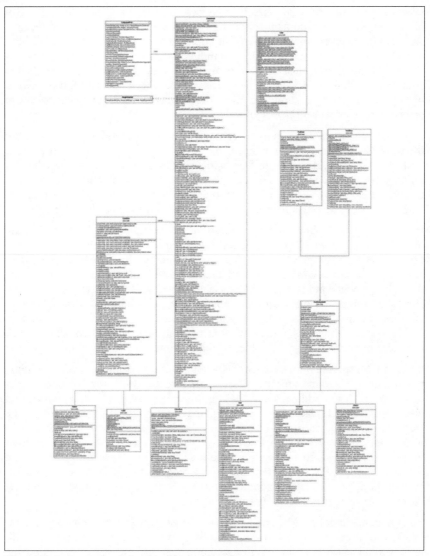

Figure 12-1. An overloaded and ineffective class diagram

Modeling Versus Diagramming

Before making Figure 12-1 more effective, let's distinguish modeling from diagramming. The act of modeling furthers your understanding of the system under study. You use diagrams to elaborate the model. You confirm the model integrity with new views. You organize your understanding. You extend your knowledge. You challenge your understanding. By seeing the known, you can infer, dictate, or investigate the yet to be known. Figure 12-1 might be seen during modeling, but only as an intermediate step; such diagrams don't demonstrate UML's true power to communicate.

Diagramming, on the other hand, expresses understanding for the benefit of others. You may be a domain expert by background, or you may have recently synthesized expertise from modeling with domain experts. You have worked hard to understand, and to put your understanding into a model, perhaps over weeks or months; now you must make that understanding immediately accessible to your readers. Your model should be concise so that they understand. If there is to be contention, let it be about real ideas, not ambiguity. *Diagramming reveals to others what you discover through modeling.*

It doesn't matter whether you formally create a model in a modeling tool, whether the model is implicitly in your head, or whether the model resides in another form: each diagram drawn from that model should express one or a very limited number of related concepts. You choose the idea to express, and you express it from the elements in the model. Presenting your ideas in UML requires multiple diagrams, just as writing a section in this chapter requires multiple paragraphs.

Implicitly, you may think that discussions of layout and effective diagrams relate only to human-drawn diagrams. Automated utilities create one-way transformations to UML of complex text or XML-based configuration files or even nontext systems. This visual UML presents an alternative and complementary view to the difficult-to-understand source text, especially when used as overviews and sanity checks. Most such utilities automatically lay out the resulting diagrams without allowing the user to arrange the diagrams. (Manual arrangement would impose undue work on the user.) The need for clarity and focus applies equally to UML produced by tools because the reader is still the same.

Though UML provides an excellent vehicle for both modeling and diagramming, the resultant diagrams aren't necessarily the same. Modeling tolerates larger diagrams with a muddled focus. A large diagram makes a better playground because the cost of refactoring many small diagrams outweighs the benefits of the clarity those diagrams provide, at least in the early stages of design. Once you understand the model and are comfortable with it, you can fission the resultant model more easily into packages and concise diagrams. Ease during this phase validates the model's completeness; pain in diagramming indicates incompleteness in modeling. Details forgotten against the vastness of the model stand out when the focus narrows to a very small context.

Your documentation, UML and otherwise, must answer when you are absent. When you're publishing a guide to a toolkit, framework, or system, your audience will fail to exploit your offering without clear and focused diagrams. At the same time, once the model is clearly understood and concisely presented, discard the playground diagrams to avoid confusion.

As with any other endeavor, shortcuts can be appropriate. If only you or an application generator access a model, you don't need to publish it for others. If the model is implicitly valid or you have better validation mechanisms, such as model checkers, you need not bother creating concise diagrams. A code generator, for example, doesn't care about understandable diagrams.

No one diagram is definitive in all aspects. To be effective, a diagram must have unity of purpose. As a 2D view of the model, a diagram necessarily leaves out details in order to emphasize important features. The more economic the details, the more salient the features appear in relief. Several diagrams, each with a different purpose, provide a clearer understanding than one diagram that has all the details.

When diagramming, consider the purpose. The following sections detail several errors that compromise the effectiveness of UML.

Structure and Interrelationships Among Classes

Figure 12-1 shows a class diagram cluttered by details. It gives no insight. Figure 12-2 shows the same classes without attributes and operations. More than half the diagram is an understandable inheritance tree. Rid now of clutter, what's left becomes readable. The converging lines draw the eye to Component at the center. You can clearly see the relationships between the abstract classes and various interfaces. The subclasses clearly add individual behavior without adding any structure. The diagram works. Once you understand the structure, you can find the details of operations and attributes elsewhere, in such places as source comment extraction tools such as Javadoc (supplied with the standard Java SDK from Sun) or CppDoc (check for it at *http://www.cppdoc.com/*).

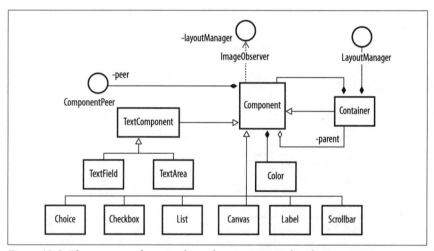

Figure 12-2. The structure of commonly used components within the Java AWT

Figure 12-2 illustrates that good diagramming doesn't need to show everything. Effective diagramming communicates one aspect of a system well. The less cluttered a diagram, the better. We chose to communicate the class structure of the Java AWT system. To that end, the diagram focuses on classes and their relationships, and leaves off details, such as attributes, which have no bearing on the knowledge we are trying to share.

Separate Inheritance and Class Interrelationships

Our subset of the AWT doesn't contain enough complexity to require more simplification. Figure 12-2 mixes the abstract class relationships and the concrete classes using them. For even more clarity, together Figures 12-3 and 12-4 illustrate the same model as do Figures 12-1 and 12-2, but they separate the two concerns of abstraction and inheritance. Figure 12-3 focuses on the abstraction common to all the Components. With just two interesting classes and four supporting classes, Figure 12-3 is simple enough to memorize. That learned, the inheritance hierarchy of concrete classes in Figure 12-4 becomes easy to classify and to manipulate.

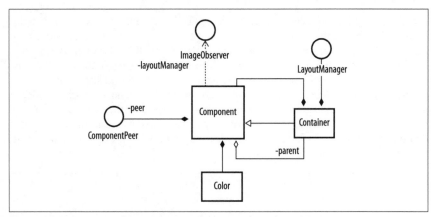

Figure 12-3. Structure of Components and Containers in the AWT

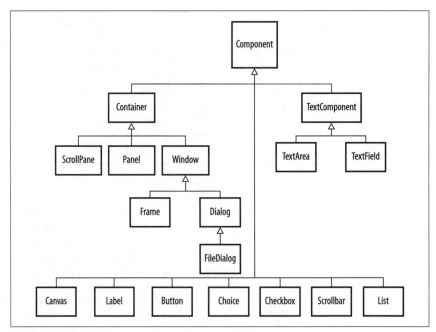

Figure 12-4. Inheritance tree of Component in the AWT

Sprawling Scope

Figure 12-5 shows an example of a poorly focused sequence diagram. Sequence diagrams risk taking on too many interactions at once. This one shows the Struts interactions, the application interactions, and then the detailed workings of the Java libraries.

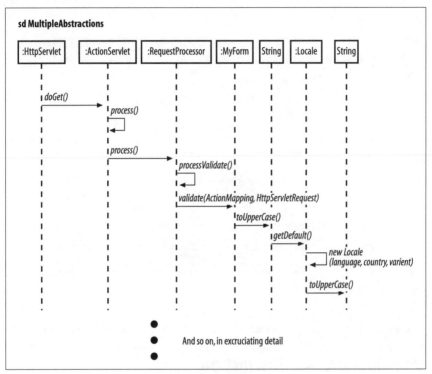

Figure 12-5. Sequence diagram of HTTP form processing, spanning Struts, application, and java.lang

Elements at the high and low end of this diagram are clearly out of scope of the application. One rarely cares how Struts, as an off-the-shelf framework, works. It calls the application logic at the appropriate time. Similarly, just how the internals of the standard libraries carry out their obligations normally doesn't matter in terms of understanding the application. Both the structure of HTTP request processing and the workings of Strings are God-given as far as the application developer is concerned. However, by showing a few elements that are out of scope, the diagram allows you to see the context of the application within the greater framework, and that's often useful when selecting an architecture. Similarly, drilling down into the base libraries exposes thread or performance issues. These are exceptional needs; there is no call to complicate the description of an application with these exploratory needs. From the readers' point of view, nonapplication elements just cloud understanding of the business logic, the only thing over which the developer exerts control.

Figure 12-6 shows the processing for another HTML form. It gets to the point. It is concise enough for one page. And it focuses on interactions between the application classes; the interactions are under control of the development team.

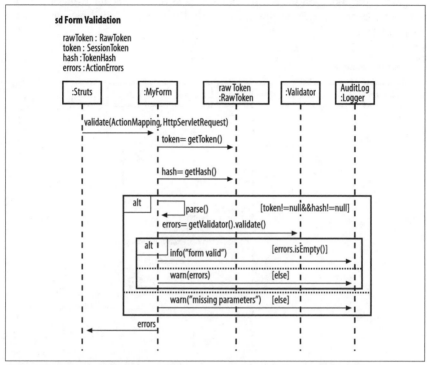

Figure 12-6. Sequence diagram with scope restricted to programmer-defined classes

One Diagram/One Abstraction

Earlier, in Figures 12-2 and 12-3, we separated structure from inheritance. Each diagram contains fewer elements than the all-encompassing diagram shown in Figure 12-1, or even the more modest one shown in Figure 12-2, so they are easier to understand. Figure 12-7 shows package dependencies. The diagram records both the import graph and code generation directives. The superimposition of these two roles results in a diagram with pairs of opposing dependencies between elements. Don't worry if you don't quite understand its meaning; we'll clean it up in a moment.

Figure 12-7 fails as a diagram for several reasons. Most strikingly, you don't know where to start: the diagram has no center of gravity. This leads to a lack of flow or direction; do you read the diagram left to right, top to bottom, or inside out? The apparently cyclic dependencies confound any sense of direction. Although opaque to the initiated, the problem with Figure 12-7 stems from trying to use one diagram for two related but different ends: controlling imports and directing code generation.

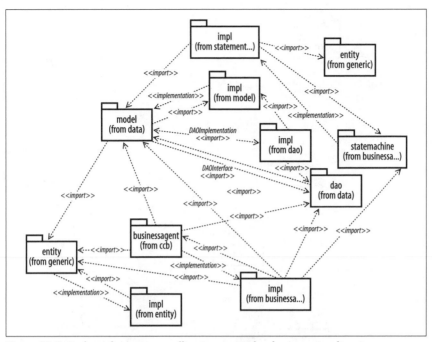

Figure 12-7. Package diagram controlling imports and code generation directives

Figure 12-8 addresses the issue of imports only. Elements higher in the diagram depend on elements below. No cycles exist. You can absorb the meaning of the diagram quickly.

Removing the imports from Figure 12-7 simplifies it more than you might imagine. Instead of forming a graph like the imports, the directives, as shown in Figure 12-9, just link separate elements with target packages. The noise of the import graph complicated a simple picture. The complicated, large diagram becomes a small diagram of four separate sections.

Besides UML

UML provides description that's difficult to match with plain text. Its formalism allows a few lines and boxes to unequivocally and immediately convey what would require time to assimilate from text. The text replaced by diagrams would be, at best, dull and legalistic, and at worst, vague, ambiguous, and open to interpretation. Either way, well-written UML is more effective.

While it may be true that a picture is worth a thousand words, a picture with words is worth much more than just a picture. Perhaps in the context of MDA and executable models, UML can provide a minimum specification for an application generator. In most cases, complete system specification or system documentation requires commentary to explain, emphasize, and give nuance to the diagrams. Diagrams alone risk burying or glossing over details as much as text alone. Diagrams and text reinforce each other. You can describe the context and

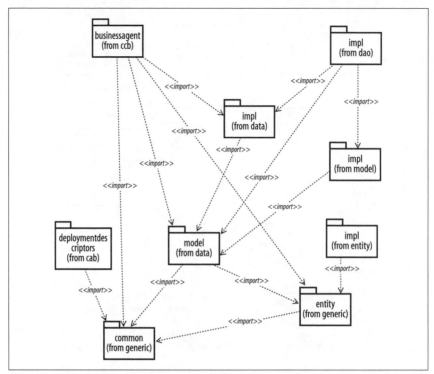

Figure 12-8. Package imports

major points with text, then drive home those points with a good diagram and the formalism of UML.

As seen throughout this chapter, you can't effectively document classes with large APIs on a single, class diagram. Hundreds of attributes and operations become insignificant on a diagram. The operation and attribute sections of a class box don't allow for descriptions. Tools such as Doxygen (*http://www.doxygen.org*) or Javadoc extract the most current source comments into searchable web pages. Though the details they present are likely to change and therefore will make diagrams obsolete, when they are made part of the software build process, they remain up to date with the latest software changes.

Remember that diagramming requires neither model nor modeling tool. UML practitioners often simply draw diagrams by hand or with simple drawing tools. Modeling tools are expensive acquisitions, in terms of time and distraction, if not in money: open source or proprietary, UML tools take time to master. White-boards, notepads, and simple drawing tools deliver much project value with no learning curve. Use them until you are comfortable with UML and its place in the project. With a firm understanding of UML and your process, choosing a dedicated UML tool and changing your process to incorporate it becomes less risky.

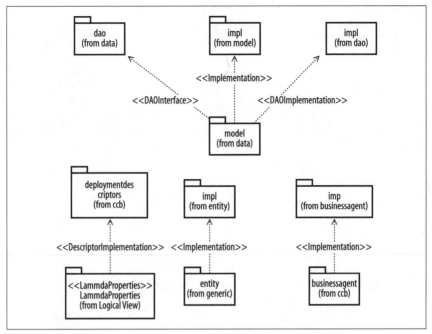

Figure 12-9. Code generation directives

A

MDA: Model-Driven Architecture

This appendix summarizes Model Driven Architecture (MDA). Several authors dedicate whole books to MDA; seek out those books. The treatment here aims simply to demystify MDA enough so that you can talk sensibly about it. Better yet, investigate the vendor offerings. Abstract descriptions don't deliver value: tools do.

 Both Model Driven Architecture and MDA, like the Unified Modeling Language and UML, are trademarks of the Object Management Group.

What Is MDA?

MDA is the natural evolution of UML, Object Oriented Analysis and Design (OOAD), code generators, and third millennium computing power. At the highest level, MDA envisions the day that UML models become the standard way to design and build software. Business software developers will build their systems through MDA tools. Development in 3GL languages such as Java or .Net will remain a toilsome necessity for the system level. For business applications, current languages will be too inefficient to be viable, used only by the most backward-looking organizations. As an analogy, consider the place of assembler and C (or even C++) in main-line business applications today.

MDA uses models to get the highest leverage out of software development. MDA isn't a development process. It isn't a specification. It isn't an implementation. It isn't a conformance suite. It doesn't have a reference implementation. The OMG, wisely, has avoided specifying how you go about leveraging software models. MDA has not matured, so each of the nearly 50 companies committed to MDA promote vastly differing visions. If you find this confusing, you aren't alone.

MDA defines a framework for processing and relating models. MDA tools transform pure business models into complete, deployable, running applications with a minimum of technological decisions. Modifying the pure business model behind an application require only updates in the dependent technological area(s). Technology decisions unrelated to the change remain, so the application can be regenerated in a matter of a few minutes.

An application has many concerns; some related to the business itself, some related to a particular implementation tier, some related to a particular implementation technology. MDA further separates the technological concerns of an application from the business; it separates high-level technical decisions from their technological implementation; it separates one technology from another. Web forms or database tactics don't complicate the business concepts of, say, Account and Customer. Transaction management decisions don't affect persistence. Messaging doesn't interfere with property management or security. Each technology can be replaced without recoding. In the extreme case, the business application can be redeployed on a completely different technology platform.

MDA keeps these separate concerns in different models, while at the same time keeping the system consistent and coherent as a whole. The concept of *account*, for example, permeates most or all of the models: business, web, database, persistence, business logic, business delegate, and code. Not only is any one model consistent within itself, but also the concepts from one model relate to the corresponding concepts in other models. Changes in the concept of *account* must affect all related models. This notion moves significantly ahead of current non-MDA modeling tools that either model everything in one model or require manual synchronization of separate models.

Although ultimately hoping to eliminate all programming languages, current MDA tools can't provide enough finesse to deliver varied and high quality systems without a hybrid approach of UML and 3GL. MDA allows handcoded extensions and other tweaking throughout the abstraction layers. It remembers the origins of these changes so that subsequent generations of the system respect them.

MDA tools are sophisticated systems. No offering has established itself as a leader. Most of the MDA offerings cater to niche markets. Most predate MDA, so they drag along baggage of a less well-defined approach, or of a well-defined but narrow proprietary approach. None manages highly abstract models *and* generates crack code *and* generates a variety of implementations, at least not yet. Though a one-size-fits-all offering doesn't exist, many offerings are very productive. The goal of MDA, while simple to voice, has yet to be fully implemented.

The Models of MDA

Models play a big role in MDA. As a framework for building systems, MDA abstracts systems into abstraction layers. Traditionally OOAD had analysis, detailed design and code roughly representing a system's business perspective, the architectural/technological perspective, and the implementation perspective. MDA adds one abstraction on top, representing the business context of the system. Figure A-1 shows the different abstraction layers and their associated MDA models. Abstraction increases toward the left and concreteness increases toward the right. Concrete models outnumber abstract models. In general, the abstract begets the concrete; as each model becomes more concrete, it realizes the abstractions with respect to one technology or platform. The inverse, making abstract models from the concrete, also known as reverse engineering, rarely happens, except when the starting point is code. Even then because the system must support a business, starting from the business needs is generally more appropriate.

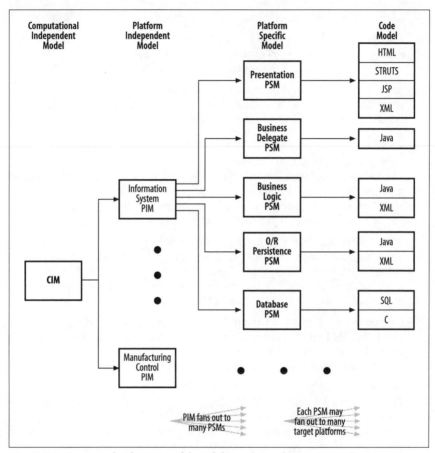

Figure A-1. An example of MDA models and their relationship

The abstraction models match well with the conceptual layers of a system:

Computational-independent model (CIM)
> The CIM represents the highest-level business model. The CIM uses a specialized business process language and not UML, although its language could well be derived from the meta-object facility (MOF).

> The CIM transcends computer systems. Each process interacts with human workers and/or machine components. The CIM describes these interactions

between these processes and the responsibilities of each worker, be it human or otherwise.

Anyone understanding business and business processes can understand a CIM. It avoids specialized knowledge of procedures internal to a worker computer system, such as accounting procedures or sales commissions.

Platform-independent model (PIM)

A PIM represents the business model to be implemented by an information system. Commonly, UML or some UML derivative describes the PIM.

The PIM describes the processes and structure of the system, without reference to the delivery platforms. The PIM ignores operating systems, programming languages, hardware, and networking.

Anyone understanding the specialized domain of the computer system under study can understand the PIM. Although destined to be an information system, the PIM requires no information system background.

The PIM is the starting point for MDA discussions in this appendix.

Platform-specific model (PSM)

The PSM projects the PIM onto a specific platform. Because one PIM begets multiple PSMs, the PSMs must collaborate to deliver a consistent and complete solution. Commonly, the implementer defines a different UML profile to define the PSM for each target platform.

The PSM realizes the PIM as it applies to one specific platform. The PSM deals explicitly with the operating system, programming language, technology platform (e.g., CORBA, .Net, J2EE, or PHP), remote distribution or local collocation. Although porting from one platform or language probably means discarding the PSM, sibling PSMs and the PIM remain unchanged.

Despite the need for an understanding of the underlying technology to understand the PSM, the understanding need not be profound. Modelers must know the difference between locally and remotely located components; they don't need to know how to implement or debug them.

Code model

The code model represents the deployable code, usually in a high-level language such as XML, Java, C#, C++, VB, HTML, JSP, or ASP. It may or may not be readable. It may or may not be extendable, although often it has extension points in the form of protected code blocks.

Ideally, the code model is compile-ready. It doesn't require any further human intervention. Deployment should be automated. In a mature MDA environment, you can think of the code model as you would think of object files or class files—they're just machine files, opaque to mere mortals.

In reality, MDA tools aren't mature. Developers need to understand the technology so that they can debug the application or the deployment. Developers need to load the source into IDEs and debug and deploy as normal. Because little code is actually handwritten, the dilemma is more to deploy correctly than to debug infrastructure.

These models can continue on to the right. We can have a bytecode or link object model, and beyond that a machine code model. Software has matured so much that the vast majority of workers take those models for granted. They just work. If they don't, we just replace them.

Figure A-1 shows a one-tier PSM. MDA doesn't restrict PSMs to one tier. Each PSM addresses a different technological layer of a system. If a particular technology lends itself to multiple layers of abstraction, the PSM allows for that too. The specific technologies, and hence, PSMs, are defined by the MDA tool and the architecture it proposes. As a business application developer, you will have to work with that particular framework.

Design Decisions

As you've seen in Figure A-1, the number of models increases as you go from the abstract to the concrete. How abstract models become transformed into more concrete models will be discussed a little later. For now, suffice it to say that some function transforms them. Several concrete models can come from a single abstract model. At any one level of abstraction, the model presents the system, without the messiness of implementation details found in the more concrete, downstream models.

Effective model transformation demands precise implementation details. Decisions at one layer imply gross differences at the next, more concrete layer. Consider the following business rules:

- There are only a few (50) states, and they don't change.

- Account transactions can be added, but never changed or deleted, and there can be hundreds of thousands of transactions for one account.

- Account balances are updated very often, but account contact information is updated relatively rarely compared to the number of times it's read. Changes must be audited.

If similar code were to be generated to manage these data entities, you would have a very poor system. To live up to its moniker, MDA must provide some clue in the business model to differentiate between these cases. The business layer doesn't involve itself with design issues such as data access patterns, but it must provide hints. These hints are *design decisions*. Models provide implicit hints through the structure (a one-to-one association versus a many-to-one association), and they can be elaborated with explicit hints (such as differentiating the three earlier cases).

At the level of code generation, 3GLs have hints, although they work at a much lower level of abstraction. Programmers switch on code optimization or debugging information. As a result, the bytecode/object code becomes vastly different, with different performance characteristics.

Figure A-2 shows how MDA records design decisions as *marks*. A transformation function uses related marks, held in a subordinate *marking model*, along with the principle model, either PIM or PSM as the case may be, to create the next, more concrete model. Partitioning the marks into separate marking models keeps the principle model pure, and the marks related to different concerns separate from each other. Were the downstream technology to change, the related marks could be dropped without disturbing the principle model.

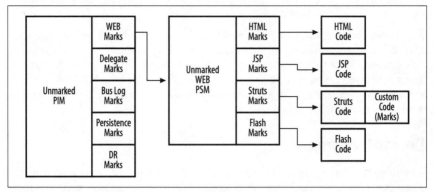

Figure A-2. Tightly coupled marking models keep technology decisions out of the principal models

Model elaboration is the intentional enrichment of a generated model. Generated models likely have need tailoring or optimization (otherwise, why have them?). Modelers assign or update the marks to control the transformation function. Programmers will add custom code in protected areas. Marks record both the updates and whether the marks originate from humans.

The unpolluted model, be it PIM or PSM, remains the same no matter how many downstream technologies there are. The principle model remains unchanged, regardless of whether a dependent model appears or disappears.

With the technology concerns partitioned from the principle model and each other, the marking models can evolve independently of each other. The technology functions can create default marks for elements. Technical modelers, who are experts in different fields, elaborate their models separately.

Sewing the Models Together

At any one time, the many models are implicitly related. For example, a transformation function transforms the PIM and related marks from a marking model to create a PSM. An MDA system of models probably has several PSMs, each with its own marking model and at least one code model, and likely its own marking model or handcoded extensions.

Over time, the PIM will change, as will the marks on it and on the PSM. If the transformation function summarily overwrites existing marks explicitly updated by a modeler, the effect of the marks disappears; the modeler must reenter all again. Clearly, this is untenable. On the other hand, deletions from the PIM will remove the justification of derived elements in the PSM. The transformation function must have a way to detect and merge collisions, and to remove deadwood. Traceability of ownership and generation becomes a serious issue.

MDA stores the relationships between source models, marks, and target models in a *mapping model*. The example in Figure A-3 shows how each element in the target model has a mapping to the source model and the appropriate marks (and, optionally, to the marking models).

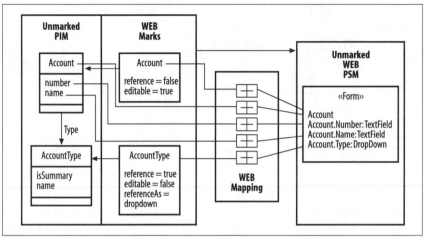

Figure A-3. Mapping models ensure traceability between the models and the marks

The mappings provide the traceability necessary for subtle evolution of the whole system. The transformation process follows the links when updating a target model from new versions of the source model or source mark model. The transformation function detects conflicts between the generated elements and the existing element added or modified by modelers. It identifies deadwood in the new target model that exists only because of now-deleted elements in the source model.

Transforming Models

The models up to now provide multiple abstractions of the system. They separate the platform concerns. They trace the origin of each element. These models are static. *Transformation functions* apply a transformation to a source model to produce a target model. Figure A-4 shows the general case of the transformation function creating or updating target models from the source model and marks. The transformation function, along with the marks and the mappings, are called the *bridge* between the two principle models.

The mapping model acts in two roles. Before the transformation, it relates the elements of the source models, together with previous versions of the target models. After the transformation, the mapping model traces the source of every target model element created or updated.

During model evolution, transformations at the PIM can cause turmoil in the PSM and code models. Because of the leverage MDA gives, slight refactoring can render the mapping model incapable of reconciling changes. If mappings are recorded by element ID, deleting an element and recreating it risks orphaning it from its marks

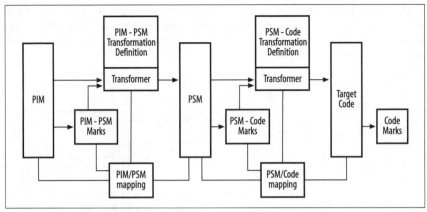

Figure A-4. Custom model transformations automate changing abstraction levels

and derivative elements in the target models. If the PSM or code model has a great deal of elaboration, MDA doesn't proscribe a solution to this.

Figure A-4 shows a transformer acting through a transformation definition. The transformer can be implemented equally well as a script or a procedural language. In any case, each transformation requires its own definition; the transformer from PIM to presentation PSM can't be reused for the database PSM to SQL code model.

The concept of reverse engineering, or round-trip engineering, received a great deal of interest a few years ago. MDA doesn't address it specifically. Each transformation function can have an inverse function to create the abstract from the concrete, but nothing requires an MDA solution to provide it.

Reverse engineering generally creates more problems than it solves. You reverse-engineer only elaborate concrete models. Concrete models may not respect the naming conventions, or they may have slight or gross variants of expected patterns. The resultant abstract model will have no insight into the structures found. Furthermore, it becomes unclear where ultimate truth lies. Remember, MDA doesn't stand for program-driven modeling.

Languages to Formally Describe MDA

The transformations describe in the preceding section can't work without strict inputs. Each model must respect a structure that constrains its expressiveness formally; automated transformations can't understand just any model. Each model requires a specialized model, as shown in Figure A-5. UML profiles provide one vehicle to constrain each model; alternative MOF-based metamodels provide another.

Explicit UML profiles enforce constraints so that only models considered valid by the transformers can be processed. Considering the leverage of expression between the PIM and each PSM, and again between each PSM and its derivative

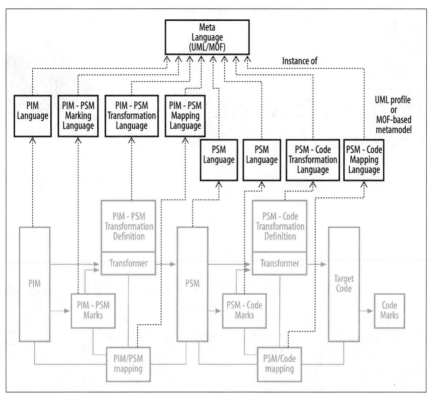

Figure A-5. Each model and transformation definition conforms to a language

code models, slightly invalid source models would produce rubbish. UML profiles provide the discipline needed to keep such a complex system running.

MDA systems need not have such a formal definition as the one we described. Certainly architects who extend the transformations with custom scripting will not back it with a formal transformation language. The languages act much as DTDs or schemas do for an XML document: languages assure that the consumers will understand the model.

B

The Object Constraint Language

The Object Constraint Language 2.0 (OCL) is an addition to the UML 2.0 specification that provides you with a way to express constraints and logic on your models. For example, you can use OCL to convey that a person's age must always be greater than 0 or that a branch office must always have one secretary for every 10 employees.

OCL isn't new to UML 2.0; it was first introduced in UML 1.4. However, as of UML 2.0, it was formalized using the Meta-Object Facility and UML 2.0. From a user's perspective the language has been updated and refined but the fundamentals remain the same. This appendix introduces the basic concepts of OCL. For more detailed information, consult the OCL specification available from the Object Management Group's web site (*http://www.omg.org/*).

OCL Basics

The Object Constraint Language is just that: a language. It obeys a syntax and has keywords. However, unlike other languages, it can't be used to express program logic or flow control. By design, OCL is a *query-only* language; it can't modify the model (or executing system) in any way. It can be used to express preconditions, postconditions, invariants (things that must always be true), guard conditions, and results of method calls.

OCL can be used virtually anywhere in UML and is typically associated with a classifier using a note. When an OCL expression is evaluated, it is considered to be instantaneous, meaning the associated classifier can't change state during the evaluation of an expression.

Basic Types

OCL has several built-in types that can be used in OCL expressions:

Boolean
Must be either true or false. Supports the logical operators and, or, xor, not, implies, and if-then-else.

Integer
Any integer value (e.g., 100, -12345, 5211976, etc.). Supports the operators *, +, -, /, and abs( ).

Real
Any decimal value (e.g., 2.222003, -67.76, etc.). Supports the operators *, +, -, /, and floor( ).

String
A series of letters, numbers, or symbols interpreted as a string (e.g., "All writing and no play make Dan..."). Supports the operators concat( ), size( ), and substring( ).

In addition to the built-in types, any classifier used in your UML model is recognized as a type by OCL. Because OCL is a strongly typed language, you can't compare values of one type directly with values of another type.

Casting

OCL does support *casting* objects from one type to another as long as they are related through a generalization relationship. To cast from one type to another use the operation *oldType*.oclAsType(*newType*). For example, to cast a Java List to an ArrayList to call the size( ) operation, use the expression:

```
List.oclAsType(ArrayList).size( )
```

If the actual object isn't an instance of the new type, the expression is considered undefined.

OCL Syntax

The remainder of this chapter uses examples from the class diagram shown in Figure B-1.

Constraints on Classifiers

Each OCL expression must have some sense of *context* that an expression relates to. Often the context can be determined by where the expression is written. For example, you can link a constraint to an element using a note. You can refer to an instance of the context classifier using the keyword self. For example, if you had a constraint on Student that their GPA must always be higher than 2.0, you can attach an OCL expression to Student using a note and refer to the GPA as follows:

```
self.GPA > 2.0
```

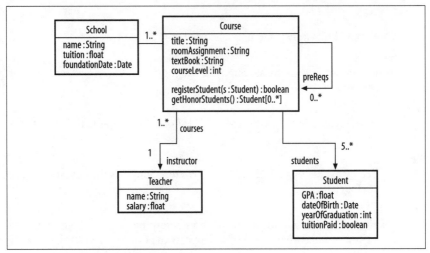

Figure B-1. Example class diagram used in this chapter

It's important to realize that this OCL expression is an invariant, meaning the system would be in an invalid state if a student's GPA dropped to less than 2.0. If you want to allow a GPA of less than 2.0 and send out a letter to the student's parents in the event such a low GPA is achieved, you would model such behavior using a UML diagram such as an activity or interaction diagram.

You can follow associations between classifiers using the association end names as though they were attributes of the originating classifier. The following invariant on Course ensures that the instructor is being paid:

```
self.instructor.salary > 0.00
```

If an association has a multiplicity of 0..1, you can treat the association end as a Set and check to see if the value is set by using the built-in notEmpty( ) operation. To call the notEmpty( ) operation on a set you must use an arrow (->) rather than a dot (.). See "Collections" for more information on sets. The following invariant on Course enforces that a course has an instructor:

```
self.instructor->notEmpty( )
```

If an association role name isn't specified, you can use the classifier name. The following invariant on School checks that each course has a room assignment:

```
self.Course->forAll(roomAssignment <> 'No room!')
```

Comments can be inserted into an expression by prefixing each comment with two dashes (--), like this:

```
-- make sure this student could graduate
self.GPA > 2.0
```

If you can't determine the context of an expression by looking at the UML model, or if you want to be explicit with the context, use the OCL keyword context, followed by the classifier name. If you use this notation, you should say what the expression represents. In the following case, we're showing an invariant, so we use the keyword inv. Other types of expressions are explained in later sections.

```
context Student
inv: self.GPA > 2.0
```

Instead of using the keyword self, you can assign a name to a classifier that you can use in the expression. Write the name you want to use, followed by a colon (:) and then the classifier name. For example, you can name the instance of Student as s:

```
context s : Student
inv: s.GPA > 2.0
```

Finally, you can name an expression by placing a label after the expression type but before the colon (:). The label is purely decorative; it serves no OCL function.

```
context s : Student
inv minimumGPARule: s.GPA > 2.0
```

Constraints on Operations

Beyond basic classifiers, OCL expressions can be associated with operations to capture preconditions and postconditions. Place the signature of the target operation (classifier, operation name, parameters, etc.) after the context keyword. Instead of the invariant keyword, use either pre or post for preconditions and postconditions, respectively.

The following expression ensures that any student who will be registered for a course has paid their tuition:

```
context Course::registerStudent(s : Student) : boolean
pre: s.tuitionPaid = true
```

When writing postconditions, you can use the keyword result to refer to the value returned by an operation. The following expressions verify that a student's tuition was paid before registering for a course and that the operation registerStudent returned true:

```
context Course::registerStudent(s : Student) : boolean
pre: s.tuitionPaid = true
post: result = true
```

As you can with invariants, you can name preconditions and postconditions by placing a label after the pre or post keywords:

```
context Course::registerStudent(s : Student) : boolean
pre hasPaidTuition: s.tuitionPaid = true
post studentWasRegistered: result = true
```

Postconditions can use the @pre keyword to refer to the value of some element *before* an operation executes. The following expression ensures that a student was registered and that the number of students in the course has increased by 1. This expression uses the self keyword to reference the object that owns the registerStudent operation.

```
context Course::registerStudent(s : Student) : boolean
pre: s.tuitionPaid = true
post: result = true AND self.students = self.students@pre + 1
```

You may specify the results of a *query* operation using the keyword body. Because OCL doesn't have syntax for program flow, you are limited to relatively simple expressions. The following expression indicates that honors students are students with GPAs higher than 3.5. The collection syntax used in this example is described in the "Collections" section.

```
context Course::getHonorsStudents( ) : Student
body: self.students->select(GPA > 3.5)
```

Constraints on Attributes

OCL expressions can specify the initial and subsequent values for attributes of classifiers. When using OCL expressions with attributes, you state the context of an expression using the classifier name, two colons (::), the attribute name, another colon (:), and then the type of the attribute. You specify the initial value of an attribute using the keyword init:

```
context School::tuition : float
init: 2500.00
```

You can specify the value of attributes after their initial value using the derive keyword. The following example increases the tuition value by 10% every time you query it:

```
context: School::tuition : float
derive: tution * 10%
```

Advanced OCL Modeling

Like any other language, OCL has an order of precedence for operators, variable declarations, and logical constructs (only for evaluating your expressions, not for program flow). The following sections describe constructs that you can use in any OCL expression.

Conditionals

OCL supports basic boolean expression evaluation using the if-then-else-endif keywords. The conditions are used only to determine which expression is evaluated; they can't be used to influence the underlying system or to affect program flow. The following invariant enforces that a student's year of graduation is valid only if she has paid her tuition:

```
context Student inv:
if tuitionPaid = true then
  yearOfGraduation = 2005
else
  yearOfGraduation = 0000
endif
```

OCL's logic rules are slightly different from typical programming language logic rules. The boolean evaluation rules are:

1. True OR-ed with anything is true.
2. False AND-ed with anything is false.
3. False IMPLIES *anything* is true.

The implies keyword evaluate the first half of an expression, and, if that first half is true, the result is taken from the second half. For example, the following expression enforces that if a student's GPA is less than 1.0, their year of graduation is set to 0. If the GPA is higher than 1.0, Rule #3 applies, and the entire expression is evaluated as true (meaning the invariant is valid).

```
context Student inv:
self.GPA < 1.0 IMPLIES self.yearOfGraduation = 0000
```

OCL's boolean expressions are valid *regardless of the order of the arguments*. Specifically, if the first argument of an AND operator is undefined, but the second operator is false, the entire expression is false. Likewise, even if one of the arguments to an OR operator is undefined, if the other is true, the expression is true. If-then-else-endif constructs are evaluated similarly; if the chosen branch can be evaluated to true or false, the nonchosen branch is completely disregarded (even if it would be undefined).

Variable Declaration

OCL supports several complex constructs you can use to make your constraints more expressive and easier to write. You can break complex expressions into reusable pieces (within the same expression) by using the let and in keywords to declare a variable. You declare a variable by giving it a name, followed by a colon (:), its type, an expression for its value, and the in keyword. The following example declares an expression that ensures a teacher of a high-level course has an appropriate salary:

```
context Course inv:
let salary : float = self.instructor.salary in
if self.courseLevel > 4000 then
  salary > 80000.00
else
  salary < 80000.00
endif
```

You can define variables that can be used in multiple expressions on a classifier-by-classifier basis using the def keyword. For example, instead of declaring salary as a variable using the let keyword, you can define it using the def keyword for the Course context. Once you define a variable using the def keyword, you may use that variable in any expression that is in the same context. The syntax for the def keyword is the same as that for the let keyword:

```
context Course
def: salary : float = self.instructor.salary
```

So, now you can write the previous invariant as:

```
context Course inv:
if self.courseLevel > 4000 then
  salary > 80000.00
getHonorsStudentselse
  salary < 80000.00
endif
```

Operator Precedence

OCL operators have the following order of precedence (from highest to lowest):

- `@pre`
- dot (.) and arrow (->) operations
- not and unary minus (-)
- `*` and `/`
- `+` and −
- `if-then-else-endif`
- `<`, `>`, `<=`, and `>=`
- `=` and `<>`
- and, or, and xor
- `implies`

You can use parentheses to group expressions, which will be evaluated from the innermost set of parentheses to the outermost.

Built-in Object Properties

OCL provides a set of properties on all objects in a system. You can invoke these properties in your expressions as you do any other properties. The built-in properties are:

`oclIsTypeOf(t : Type)` : Boolean
    Returns true if the tested object is exactly the same type as *t*.

`oclIsKindOf(t : Type)` : Boolean
    Returns true if the tested object is the same type or a subtype of *t*.

`oclInState(s : State)` : Boolean
    Returns true if the tested object is in state *s*. The states you can test must be part of a state machine attached to the classifier being tested.

`oclIsNew( )` : Boolean
    Designed to be used in a postcondition for an operation, it returns true if the object being tested was created as a result of executing the operation.

`oclAsType (t : Type)` : Type
    Returns the owning object casted to *Type*. If the object isn't a descendant of *t*, the operation is undefined.

Here are some examples of the built-in properties:

```
-- test that the instructor is an instance of Teacher
context Course
inv: self.instructor.oclIsTypeOf(Teacher)

-- cast a Date class to a java.sql.Date to verify the minutes
-- (it's very unlikely the foundationDate would be a java.sql.Date
-- so this invariant would be undefined, but this is an example
-- of using oclAsType())
context School
inv: self.foundationDate.oclAsType(java.sql.Date).getMinutes() = 0
```

Collections

OCL defines several types of collections that represent several instances of a classifier. The basic type is Collection, which is the base class for the other OCL collection classes. Quite a few operations are defined for Collection; see the OCL specification for the complete list.

All collections support a way to select or reject elements using the operations select() and reject(), respectively. To invoke an operation on a collection, you use an arrow (->) rather than a dot (.) (a dot accesses a property). The result of select or reject is another collection containing the appropriate elements. Remember that since OCL can't modify a system in any way, the original collection is unchanged. The notation for a select is:

```
collection->select(boolean expression)
```

So, to select students with GPAs higher than 3.0, you can use the expression:

```
context Course::getHonorsStudents() : Student
body: self.students->select(GPA > 3.0)
```

Or, to eliminate honor students that haven't paid their tuition:

```
context Course::getHonorsStudents() : Student
body: self.students->select(GPA > 3.0)->reject(tuitionPaid = false)
```

In the previous examples, the context for the select and reject statements was implied. You can explicitly name the element you want to use in the boolean expression by prefixing the expression with a label and a pipe symbol (|). So, a rewrite of the GPA example using a label to identify each student looks like this:

```
context Course::getHonorsStudents() : Student
body: self.students->select(curStudent | curStudent.GPA > 3.0)
```

Finally, you can specify the type of the element you want to evaluate. You indicate the type by placing a colon (:) and the classifier type after the label. Each element of the collection you are evaluating must be of the specified type, or else the expression is undefined. You can rewrite the GPA example to be even more specific and require that it evaluate only Students:

```
context Course::getHonorsStudents() : Student
body: self.students->select(curStudent : Student | curStudent.GPA > 3.0)
```

Often you will need to express a constraint across an entire collection of objects, so OCL provides the forAll operation that returns true if a given Boolean expression evaluates to true for all of the elements in a collection. The syntax for forAll is the same as that for select and reject. So, you can write a constraint that enforces that all students in a Course have paid their tuition:

```
context Course
inv: self.students->forAll(tuitionPaid = true)
```

As you can with select, you can name and type the variable used in the expression:

```
context Course
inv: self.students->forAll(curStudent : Student | curStudent.tuitionPaid =
true)
```

If you need to check to see if there is at least one element in a collection that satisfies a boolean expression, you can use the operation exists. The syntax is the same as that for select. The following expression ensures that at least one of the students has paid their tuition:

```
context Course
inv: self.students->exists(tuitionPaid = true)
```

Like select, you can name and type the variables used in the expression:

```
context Course
inv: self.students->exists(curStudent : Student | curStudent.tuitionPaid =
true)
```

You can check to see if a collection is empty using the operations isEmpty or notEmpty. The following expression ensures that the school has at least one course offering:

```
context School
inv: self.Course->notEmpty( )
```

Index

We'd like to hear your suggestions for improving our indexes. Send email to *index@oreilly.com*.

expressions
- attributes and, 196
- comments in, 194
- context of, 193, 194, 196
- declaring, 197
- evaluating, 196, 197
- grouping, 198
- as invariants, 194
- naming, 195
- naming elements, 199
- OCL and, 192, 193, 196
- operations and, 195
- undefined, 199
- variables in, 200

extend keyword, 84
extended keyword, 98
extends keyword, 84
extension
- state machines, 98
- use case, 82, 84–86

extension points, 84, 85
<<external>> keyword, 118
external state, 96
extra-global combined fragments, 152

F

final state, 92, 95
floor( ) operation, 193
flow final nodes, 117
focus of control, 6, 111, 136
forAll operation, 200
foreign keys, 36
fork and join pseudostate, 100
fork nodes, 116, 158
forward slash (/)
- deferred events, 102
- derived notation, 15
- OCL operator, 193, 198
- property instances and, 54
found messages, 134, 135
4+1 views, 7
functions, 20

G

gates, 151
general ordering, 143
generalization relationship
- casting and, 193
- defined, 28

package merging and, 42
representation, 28
generalization, use case and actor, 82
graphical representation, 166
greater than (>), 198
guard condition
- brackets and, 90
- communication diagrams, 158
- decision nodes and, 114
- edges and, 111
- interaction fragments and, 140
- interaction operators and, 141–148
- ordering, 114
- syntax, 140
- transitions, 94, 95
guillemots «», 167

H

high-level transition, 94
HyperModel, 174
hyphen (-)
- arguments and, 150
- messages, 132
- visibility, 13, 19

I

if-then-else logical operator, 193
if-then-else-endif keywords, 196
if-then-else-endif operator, 198
ignore interaction operator, 146, 147
implementation
- defined, 69
- functionality and, 82
- state machines and, 87
implementation diagrams, 165
implementation view, 8
implicit binding, 33
implies keyword, 197
implies logical operator, 193, 197, 198
<<import>> keyword, 40
importing packages, 40, 41
in keyword, 197
inactive state, 90
include keyword, 84
includes keyword, 84
inclusion, use case, 82–84
indirect substates, 92
inheritance
- classes and, 24
- decomposition and, 152

inheritance (*continued*)
  depicting, 175–176
  multiple, 28
init keyword, 196
initial nodes, 114
initial pseudostate, 92, 100
inlined attributes, 12–14
inout keyword, 132, 150
input pins
  expansion regions, 122
  object nodes and, 113
  representation, 113
  streaming, 124
instances
  artifact, 68
  collaboration, 56
  collaboration occurrences as, 57
  collections and, 199
  composite structures and, 54
  connectors and, 48
  defined, 11, 12
  interactions and, 129
  lifelines and, 131
  multiple, 108
  operations and, 23
  relative times, 160
  representation, 12
  XML documents as, 34
instantiation, 78
integer datatype, 193
interaction diagrams
  alternate notations, 155–162
  combined fragments, 139–148
  continuations, 153–155
  decomposition, 150–153
  deployment view and, 7
  event occurrences, 138
  example, 194
  execution occurrences, 136
  implementation view and, 8
  interaction occurrences, 149, 150
  interactions, 128, 129
  messages, 131–135
  participants, 129–131
  process view and, 8
  sequence timing, 155
  state invariants, 137
  traces, 139
  use case view and, 8
  use cases and, 78

interaction fragments
  communication diagrams and, 156
  defined, 139
  event occurrences and, 139
  gates and, 151
  guard conditions and, 140, 141
  messages and, 136, 140, 146, 147
  options and, 141
  parallel execution, 142–144
interaction occurrences, 149, 150
interaction operands
  breaks, 141
  critical, 140
  defined, 139
  parallel execution, 142–144
  weak sequencing, 144
interaction operators
  defined, 139
  guard conditions, 140
  messages and, 136
interaction overview diagrams, 6, 128,
      158
interaction points, 52, 53
interactions
  alternate notations, 155–162
  copying, 149
  overview, 128, 129
  participants, 129–131
  sequence diagrams and, 177
<<interface>> keyword, 30
interfaces
  black-box view, 60
  as classifiers, 30–32
  collaborations and, 56
  connection points and, 89
  dependencies, 62
  ports and, 50, 51
  representation, 30
  SPEM and, 165
  white-box view, 63
  (see also provided interfaces;
        required interfaces)
internal activities compartment, 90
internal transitions, 90, 95
interruptible activity regions, 125
inv keyword (OCL), 195
invariant condition, 89
invariants
  assertions and, 147
  constraints as, 155
  expressions as, 194

modeling (*continued*)
  diagrams, 5–7
  exception handling, 120
  notes, 8
  overview, 164–166
  static, xii
  UML and, 4
  use cases, 82–86
  views, 7, 8
models
  connecting, 188–189
  diagrams versus, 173–175
  MDA, 184–187
  OCL, 192, 196–200
  transforming, 189–190
MOF (Meta-Object Facility)
  CIM and, 185
  example, 164
  functionality, 165
  OCL and, 192
<<multicast>> keyword, 108
multicasting, 108
multidimensional partitions, 120
multiplicity
  aggregation and, 27
  associations and, 26, 30, 194
  of attributes, 12–17
  compositions and, 28
  connector ends, 50
  generalization relationships and, 28
  port, 52
  properties, 54
  representation, 16, 26, 54
  XML elements and, 34
multiplicity element (operations), 20
<<multireceive>> keyword, 108

N

name compartment, 89
name element (operations), 19
names
  association classes and, 29
  attribute syntax element, 13, 14
  connectors and, 48
  elements, 199
  postcondition, 195
  precondition, 195
  qualifying, 40
  state, 89
  use cases and, 77, 78
  variable, 197, 200

naming conventions
  abstract classes, 12, 24
  associations, 26
  concrete models and, 190
  operations, 19
  parameters, 20
navigability
  aggregation and, 27
  associations and, 26
  compositions and, 28
neg interaction operator, 145
nesting
  devices, 72
  message calls, 157
  stereotypes, 167
nodes
  activity, 111–118
  artifacts and, 73
  central buffer, 125
  data store, 126–127
  defined, 67
  exception handling, 121
  overview, 69–73
  representation, 69, 105
not logical operator, 193
not operator, 198
notEmpty( ) operation, 194, 200
notes
  modeling and, 8
  specifying constraints in, 49
  state invariants and, 137
number datatype, 168

O

Object Constraint Language (see OCL)
object diagrams
  defined, 6
  design view and, 7
  unnamed objects in, 12
object flows, 108–109
Object Management Group (see OMG)
object nodes, 113
Object Oriented Analysis and Design
  (OOAD), 183, 184
objects
  abstract classes and, 24
  actions and, 137
  built-in properties, 198
  casting, 193
  constraints and, 200
  defined, 11, 12

W

wallpaper diagrams, 172–176
weak sequencing, 144
weights, edges and, 111
white-box view (components), 60,
       63–65
whole-part relationships, 27, 28, 53

X

XML documents, 34, 191
XML Structure Definition Language
       (XSDL), 34
xor constraint, 15
xor logical operator, 193, 198
XSDL (XML Structure Definition
       Language), 34

About the Authors

Dan Pilone is a software architect with Blueprint Technologies, Inc., cofounder and president of Zizworks, Inc., and a terrible rock climber. He has designed and implemented systems for Hughes, ARINC, UPS, and the Naval Research Laboratory. When not writing for O'Reilly, he teaches software design and software engineering at the Catholic University in Washington, D.C. He is the author of the *UML Pocket Reference* and has had several articles published covering software process, consulting in the software industry, and 3D graphics in Java.

Neil Pitman is chief technical officer of Mahjong Mania, codeveloper of LamMDA from Mindset Corporation, and formerly vice president of research and development at Codagen Technologies. Neil has 20 years of experience in software development ranging from medical systems to Smalltalk development platforms, gaming software to code generation. When he does real work, it's in J2EE and XSLT as well as UML. Look for him at *http://www.architecturerules.com*.

Colophon

Our look is the result of reader comments, our own experimentation, and feedback from distribution channels. Distinctive covers complement our distinctive approach to technical topics, breathing personality and life into potentially dry subjects.

The animal on the cover of *UML 2.0 in a Nutshell* is a chimpanzee (*Pan troglodytes*). Chimpanzees use a vast array of facial expressions, postures, and gestures to communicate with each other, in addition to at least 32 different sounds. There is some evidence to suggest that chimpanzees can learn symbolic languages.

The natural habitat of the chimpanzee is western Africa, from Sierra Leone to the Great Lakes east of the Congo. Living primarily in forested areas, chimpanzees spend 50 to 70 percent of their time in trees. They are omnivores, eating primarily fruits and vegetables, but they will also hunt and eat small animals. They live in family groups that consist of about twice as many females as males. While adult chimpanzees aren't monogamous, there's a close bond between a young chimp and its parents, and this bond remains unbroken for life. Chimpanzees are very sociable and affectionate animals, and frequently hug, kiss, stroke each other, or hold hands. Violent fights often break out within a social group. The loser of the fight makes up to the winner by displaying submissive behavior and conciliatory gestures. In this way they maintain the social harmony.

Though able to, the chimpanzee rarely walks erect on both feet. Short arm muscles prevent simultaneous extension of the wrists and fingers. Because of this, chimpanzees can't walk with their hands flat; when walking on all fours, only the knuckles of their hands touch the ground. Unlike human feet, chimpanzee feet also have an opposing toe, but it's used mainly for climbing and for walking on precarious footing. The foot is rarely used for picking up objects.

Mary Anne Weeks Mayo was the production editor and proofreader, and Audrey Doyle was the copyeditor for *UML 2.0 in a Nutshell*. Phil Dangler and Colleen Gorman provided quality control. Peter Ryan provided production assistance. Lucie Haskins wrote the index.

Ellie Volckhausen designed the cover of this book, based on a series design by Edie Freedman. The cover image is a 19th-century engraving from the Dover Pictorial Archive. Karen Montgomery produced the cover layout with Adobe InDesign CS using Adobe's ITC Garamond font.

David Futato designed the interior layout. This book was converted by Keith Fahlgren to FrameMaker 5.5.6 with a format conversion tool created by Erik Ray, Jason McIntosh, Neil Walls, and Mike Sierra that uses Perl and XML technologies. The text font is Linotype Birka; the heading font is Adobe Myriad Condensed; and the code font is LucasFont's TheSans Mono Condensed. The illustrations that appear in the book were produced by Robert Romano, Jessamyn Read, and Lesley Borash using Macromedia FreeHand MX and Adobe Photoshop CS. The tip and warning icons were drawn by Christopher Bing. This colophon was written by Clairemarie Fisher O'Leary.

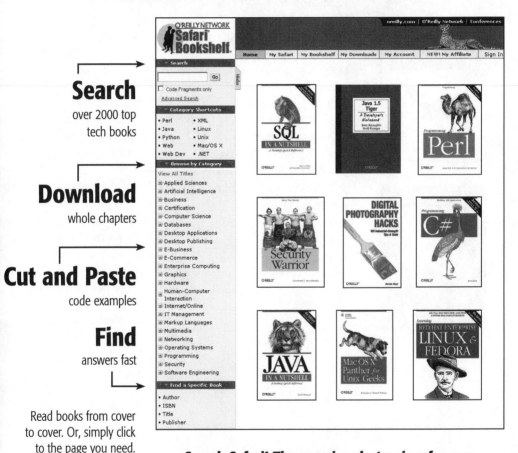

Part# 40421

Related Titles Available from O'Reilly

Java

Ant: The Definitive Guide

Better, Faster, Lighter Java

Eclipse

Eclipse Cookbook

Enterprise JavaBeans,
4th Edition

Hardcore Java

Head First Java

Head First Servlets & JSP

Head First EJB

Hibernate:
A Developer's Notebook

J2EE Design Patterns

Java 1.5 Tiger:
A Developer's Notebook

Java & XML Data Binding

Java & XML

Java Cookbook, 2nd Edition

Java Data Objects

Java Database Best Practices

Java Enterprise Best Practices

Java Enterprise in a Nutshell,
2nd Edition

Java Examples in a Nutshell,
3rd Edition

Java Extreme Programming
Cookbook

Java in a Nutshell, 4th Edition

Java Management Extensions

Java Message Service

Java Network Programming,
2nd Edition

Java NIO

Java Performance Tuning,
2nd Edition

Java RMI

Java Security, 2nd Edition

JavaServer Faces

Java ServerPages, 2nd Edition

Java Servlet & JSP Cookbook

Java Servlet Programming,
2nd Edition

Java Swing, 2nd Edition

Java Web Services in a Nutshell

Learning Java, 2nd Edition

Mac OS X for Java Geeks

Programming Jakarta Struts
2nd Edition

Tomcat: The Definitive Guide

WebLogic:
The Definitive Guide

O'REILLY®

Our books are available at most retail and online bookstores.
To order direct: 1-800-998-9938 • order@oreilly.com • www.oreilly.com
Online editions of most O'Reilly titles are available by subscription at safari.oreilly.com

Keep in touch with O'Reilly

1. Download examples from our books

To find example files for a book, go to:
www.oreilly.com/catalog
select the book, and follow the "Examples" link.

2. Register your O'Reilly books

Register your book at *register.oreilly.com*

Why register your books? Once you've registered your O'Reilly books you can:

- Win O'Reilly books, T-shirts or discount coupons in our monthly drawing.
- Get special offers available only to registered O'Reilly customers.
- Get catalogs announcing new books (US and UK only).
- Get email notification of new editions of the O'Reilly books you own.

3. Join our email lists

Sign up to get topic-specific email announcements of new books and conferences, special offers, and O'Reilly Network technology newsletters at:

elists.oreilly.com

It's easy to customize your free elists subscription so you'll get exactly the O'Reilly news you want.

4. Get the latest news, tips, and tools

http://www.oreilly.com

- "Top 100 Sites on the Web"—PC Magazine
- CIO Magazine's Web Business 50 Awards

Our web site contains a library of comprehensive product information (including book excerpts and tables of contents), downloadable software, background articles, interviews with technology leaders, links to relevant sites, book cover art, and more.

5. Work for O'Reilly

Check out our web site for current employment opportunities:

jobs.oreilly.com

6. Contact us

O'Reilly & Associates
1005 Gravenstein Hwy North
Sebastopol, CA 95472 USA

TEL: 707-827-7000 or 800-998-9938
(6am to 5pm PST)

FAX: 707-829-0104

order@oreilly.com
For answers to problems regarding your order or our products.
To place a book order online, visit:
www.oreilly.com/order_new

catalog@oreilly.com
To request a copy of our latest catalog.

booktech@oreilly.com
For book content technical questions or corrections.

corporate@oreilly.com
For educational, library, government, and corporate sales.

proposals@oreilly.com
To submit new book proposals to our editors and product managers.

international@oreilly.com
For information about our international distributors or translation queries. For a list of our distributors outside of North America check out:
international.oreilly.com/distributors.html

adoption@oreilly.com
For information about academic use of O'Reilly books, visit:
academic.oreilly.com

O'REILLY®

Our books are available at most retail and online bookstores.
To order direct: 1-800-998-9938 • *order@oreilly.com* • *www.oreilly.com*
Online editions of most O'Reilly titles are available by subscription at *safari.oreilly.com*